STATE OF
THE UNION

ACTING EDITION

BY HOWARD LINDSAY AND RUSSEL CROUSE

COMEDY IN THREE ACTS

**DRAMATISTS
PLAY SERVICE
INC.**

SPECIAL NOTE
Anyone receiving permission to produce STATE OF THE UNION is required
to give credit to the Author as sole and exclusive Author of the Play on the title
page of all programs distributed in connection with performances of the Play
and in all instances in which the title of the Play appears for purposes of
advertising, publicizing or otherwise exploiting the Play and/or a production
thereof. The name of the Author must appear on a separate line, in which no
other name appears, immediately beneath the title and in size of type equal to
50% of the largest, most prominent letter used for the title of the Play. No
person, firm or entity may receive credit larger or more prominent than that
accorded the Author.

STATE OF THE UNION was produced by Leland Hayward at the Hudson Theatre, New York City, November 14, 1945, with the following cast:

(In the order in which they speak)

JAMES CONOVER .... Minor Watson
SPIKE MACMANUS .... Myron McCormick
KAY THORNDYKE .... Kay Johnson
GRANT MATTHEWS .... Ralph Bellamy
NORAH .... Helen Ray
MARY MATTHEWS .... Ruth Hussey
STEVENS .... John Rowe
BELLBOY .... Howard Graham
WAITER .... Robert Toms
SAM PARRISH .... Herbert Heyes
SWENSON .... Fred Ayres Cotton
JUDGE JEFFERSON DAVIS ALEXANDER .... G. Albert Smith
MRS. ALEXANDER .... Maidel Turner
JENNY .... Madeline King
MRS. DRAPER .... Aline McDermott
WILLIAM HARDY .... Victor Sutherland
SENATOR LAUTERBACK .... George Lessey

SCENES

ACT I

SCENE 1: The study in James Conover's home in Washington, D. C. A small room.[1]

SCENE 2: A bedroom in the Conover home. The following evening.

ACT II

The living-room of a suite in the Book-Cadillac Hotel, Detroit. Several weeks later.

ACT III

SCENE 1: The living-room of the Matthews apartment in New York. Two weeks later.

SCENE 2: The same—an hour later.

[1] Note on staging: The authors suggest that the play may be given in three sets, rather than four, by playing Scene 1 in the bedroom set which is also used for Scene 2.

The political comment in this play reflects the issues of the year 1946. It would not be difficult for anyone politically informed to bring these issues up-to-date by re-writing the lines involved. This would in no way affect the structure of the play or qualify its basic story. However, if this is done there must be a program note giving credit to whoever makes these revisions and absolving Mr. Lindsay and Mr. Crouse of any responsibility for the political implications contained in the revised version.

STATE OF THE UNION

ACT I

SCENE 1

The study in the home of JAMES CONOVER *in* Washington, D. C.

DISCOVERED: JAMES CONOVER, *a quiet-spoken man of about 60, of good appearance, not quite the type the audience would expect as a politician. Seated near him is* MRS. KATHERINE THORNDYKE, *known hereafter as* KAY, *a handsome woman in her late thirties. She is the kind you would find talking to men more often than women. Seated upstage is* SPIKE MACMANUS. *He has been for years a* Washington *political reporter, pudgy and genial and with a rough charm. He knows how to make friends and influence people. Seated across the room from* KAY *and* CONOVER *is* GRANT MATTHEWS, *a distinguished looking man in his middle forties, a successful business man, but also much more than that.*

AT RISE: JAMES CONOVER *is seated to* R. *of the desk engaged in a telephone conversation. His share of the conversation consists almost entirely of listening, with an occasional murmur of assent. The other three are obviously waiting for him to finish and have no interest in what is being said on the telephone. Their attention wanders away from* CONOVER *to themselves.* KAY *consults her handbag mirror and passes her hand over her hair.* SPIKE *takes a paper out of his pocket, glances at some notes on it and puts it back in his pocket.* KAY *looks toward* GRANT *and, when their eyes meet, she smiles and nods an indication that everything is going all right. In reply* GRANT *shrugs noncommittally. They both look at* SPIKE, *who makes a reassuring gesture with his hands, palms down.* CONOVER *interrupts the flow of conversation over the telephone, speaking with quiet authority.*

CONOVER. (*Into phone.*) Uh-huh. Yes. Dave, I'm sorry, but I have to give the Senator a free hand in this. (*Pause.*) Has this occurred to you? The reason you and the Senator are fighting over this one appointment is because we lost the last election and the one before that and the one before that! We have to win the next one! The Senator feels that appointment will strengthen the party in his district. So there's no argument. (*Short pause.*) Certainly, any time. Good night, Dave. (*He hangs up.*)

SPIKE. You're being pretty tough on Tisdale, Jim. If he can't swing that appointment, how's he going to stay out of jail?

CONOVER. Spike, you know too much.

SPIKE. (*Grinning.*) I've been blackmailing Tisdale for years. He's one of my best sources.

CONOVER. Spike's just trying to show off in front of his boss, Mrs. Thorndyke.

KAY. He doesn't have to. I'm not the only publisher who thinks Spike's the best newspaper man in Washington.

CONOVER. (*Mockingly.*) Well—I think Walter Lippmann writes a little better.

KAY. Oh, we wouldn't let Spike write a paragraph.

SPIKE. They even took away my typewriter—but they gave me six telephones.

KAY. Spike knows more about what's going on in Washington than you and Bob Hannagan put together. That's why I'm willing to lend him to you for the campaign—but I want him back!

CONOVER. (*Half kidding.*) Too bad you weren't running Dewey's campaign, Spike.

SPIKE. Well, if Dewey had listened to me when I saw him in Albany he'd have had a much better chance. (*The others look at* SPIKE *with smiling disbelief.*) I didn't say he'd have had a chance. I said he'd have had a much better chance.

KAY. (*To* CONOVER.) Jim, do you think you're going to have trouble stopping Dewey?

CONOVER. (*Quietly.*) I won't have to stop him. The other candidates will do that.

SPIKE. The Republicans never have nominated a defeated candidate. That's on the record. The boys feel that way about Dewey, don't they, Jim?

CONOVER. I can't speak for the Republican party ——

SPIKE. Hell, who can these days? It's going to be a dogfight. But if

6

there's a *deadlock* in the convention that gives you a chance to name your own man.

KAY. If we get a strong candidate in '48 we've got better than a fighting chance. Jim, my newspapers are city papers, but small cities, with a rural circulation, too. They make a pretty good sounding board. Here's what comes back to me. The party's best chance in '48 is to put up a candidate who's never been identified with politics.

SPIKE. Look what happened in '40. If the election had been held a month after Philadelphia, Willkie would have won.

KAY. Yes, and why? Because the people had the idea Willkie was somebody you politicians didn't want.

SPIKE. (*To* CONOVER.) You wouldn't mind if that impression got around about the candidate in '48, would you?

CONOVER. Not if the candidate was somebody I *did* want.

SPIKE. That's what I mean.

CONOVER. It seems to me at this point we ought to hear from Mr. Matthews. (*They all look at* GRANT.)

GRANT. Let me make this clear—I don't want to be President of the United States. (*They smile at his vehemence.*)

CONOVER. I don't know why any man wants to be President. That decision may not be in your hands.

GRANT. Mr. Conover, I can understand Mrs. Thorndyke telling me I should be President. But—you must be talking about somebody else.

CONOVER. You're a national figure—and you have been ever since the war!

KAY. Grant, everybody in the country knows you and everybody respects you.

GRANT. Oh, they know I make good airplanes and I've made a hell of a lot of them.

SPIKE. They know more than that. (*He rises and crosses to* GRANT.) Even when the war was on you used to crowd it off the front page. How about that time you talked back to the Senate Investigating Committee? Look at the headlines you got three months ago when you settled that strike in your plants before it got started.

CONOVER. Mrs. Thorndyke and I aren't the only Republicans who've been thinking about you. Those speeches you've been making—especially that last one in Cleveland.

GRANT. (*Placing glass on table.*) When I made that speech in Cleveland I was trying to put both parties on the spot. I wasn't speaking as a Republican. I was speaking as a citizen. I'm worried about what's happening in this country. We're splitting apart. Business, labor, farmers, cattlemen, lumbermen—they're all trying to get the biggest bite of the apple. No wonder prices are sky high. (*Rises and crosses to* C.) You talk about the danger of another war—well, we've got a war on here at home now—a civil war—an economic war. That's what I said in Cleveland. That's why I was surprised you asked me down here.

CONOVER. Why were you surprised?

GRANT. Because you politicians are trying to make capital out of this situation—you appeal to each one of these pressure groups just to get their votes. But let me tell you something. I don't think that's good politics. (*Crosses* L.) A lot of people wrote me after that speech in Cleveland. (*With a grin. Crosses and turns back.*) Of course I will admit that the business men liked best what I said about labor, and the unions said I was absolutely right about big business, and the farmers were pretty pleased with what I said about everybody but the farmers. But they all knew what I was talking about. They know we've all got to work in harness, if we're going to take our place in this world. And if we don't there won't be any world. (*Crosses to* KAY'S *chair.*) We may be kidding ourselves that our party is going to win in '48—but if our party does win, whoever is President has to have guts enough to pull us together and keep us together. I'm for that man, Mr. Conover—I don't care who he is. (*Turns and starts back.*)

KAY. That man is you, Grant.

GRANT. You're prejudiced, Kay. (*To* CONOVER.) The boys who fought the war deserve something better —— (*A knock on the door.*)

CONOVER. Go ahead—finish.

GRANT. No, that may be important. (*Crossing* L. *to table against* L. *wall as* SPIKE *goes to* U. S. *end of table and puts out cigarette in ashtray.*)

CONOVER. Come in. (NORAH, *a middle-aged maid, wearing glasses, enters. She has a slip of paper in her hand.*)

NORAH. (*Crossing to back of desk.*) I'm sorry to interrupt you. It's a telephone call. (*She hands* CONOVER *the slip of paper. He looks at it.*)

CONOVER. Thank you. You go to bed, Norah. I'll take the rest of the calls myself.

NORAH. (*Starting out.*) Thank you, Mr. Conover. (*Turns back at door.*) It's turned cool. I've put an extra blanket in your room, Mrs. Thorndyke. Yours, too, Mr. Matthews.

GRANT. Thank you, Norah. Good night.

KAY. Good night, Norah. (NORAH *exits.*)

CONOVER. I'll try to make this short. (*He picks up phone and speaks.*) Hello, there! How are you? (*Pause.*) Oh—can you call me on that in the morning? (*Pause.*) Well, hold on. I'll have to take this in another room. Spike MacManus is here. (CONOVER *rises, holding phone.* SPIKE *crosses to above desk, reaching for phone.*)

SPIKE. I'll hang up as soon as you're on.

CONOVER. (*Giving* SPIKE *a look, then extending phone to* KAY.) Do you mind, Mrs. Thorndyke? (KAY *rises, taking phone.* CONOVER *crosses up to door, speaks at door.*) Spike has a little Drew Pearson blood. (CONOVER *exits.* SPIKE *crosses back of* D. R. *chair.* GRANT *crosses* U. R.)

SPIKE. (*To* KAY.) If he doesn't want me to hear that, it's something we ought to hear.

KAY. (*Watching* SPIKE.) Are you on? All right, I'll hang up. (*To amuse* SPIKE *she listens for a moment before putting phone in cradle.* GRANT *has been pacing the room nervously.*)

GRANT. (*Crossing back to* L. C.) I've never felt so uncomfortable in my life. When he comes back I'm going to tell him to drop the whole subject.

KAY. (*Crossing to* GRANT.) Now, I didn't come all the way to Washington to tell Jim Conover not to talk about something we came down here to talk about. (SPIKE *sits down in* CONOVER'S *chair, picks up " Who's Who " and opens it.*)

GRANT. (*Taking* KAY'S *hands in his.*) Now, Kay, we had a lot of fun between ourselves dreaming about all this—but damn it, to ask a man like Conover to take it seriously —— (*He crosses to chair* D. L.)

KAY. (*Crossing to* GRANT, *pushing him into chair.*) Now, Grant, behave yourself. Jim Conover and I are going to talk about you and you're going to sit right down there and listen. (GRANT *looks up and grins.*)

9

GRANT. All right, I'll listen. But if Conover is serious about considering me, the Republican party must be pretty desperate.

SPIKE. (*Looking up from book.*) Oh, the Republican party isn't desperate! It's just Conover. He figures the other candidates will kill each other off, so he's looking for a dark horse.

GRANT. But Conover—he's always played along with the reactionaries. Why should he be interested in me?

SPIKE. He doesn't care what color the horse is—just so it's dark. If Conover isn't the guy who picks the Republican candidate in '48, he might as well turn Democrat.

KAY. You know, Grant, the last thing he has to boast about is Warren Harding. (SPIKE *is studying book in his lap.*)

SPIKE. And don't think he isn't serious about you! There was a book-mark in this "Who's Who" at your page. (*He looks at* GRANT.) Are you 47 years old? You don't look it. (*Looks back at book.*) You know this even impresses me. (*He runs his finger down a page.*) Twelve boards of directors! Say, there's a lot of swell angles about you!—for instance, Honorary President of the Society for the Preservation of Wild Life. (*He puts book on desk.*) How can we use that in the campaign?

KAY. (*Crossing to her chair L. of desk and sitting.*) Spike, I don't think the wild life vote is very important.

SPIKE. No, I mean from a publicity angle. Say, for instance, a picture in *Life*. (*He points to* GRANT.) You and a grateful duck. (CONOVER *enters.*)

CONOVER. (*Crossing to table L. wall.*) After that call I need a drink.

SPIKE. (*Pointing to phone.*) Oh, Senator Taft?

CONOVER. (*Laughs, then turns to mix drink.*) Anyone else?

SPIKE. I'll tend bar. (SPIKE *crosses to table L., mixes drinks and serves them during following.*)

CONOVER. Oh, thank you.

KAY. (*To* CONOVER.) Jim, do you really think Taft's serious about being a candidate himself?

CONOVER. (*Crossing to* KAY.) You can always figure that Senator Taft is serious. (*He crosses down R. to chair and sits.*) He'll go into the convention with Ohio and some Southern delegations.

SPIKE. And a knife in his back pocket. The Republicans still have time to cut each other's throats and they have always been pretty good at that.

10

KAY. Well, we can be sure of one thing. We can depend on the administration to keep on making mistakes.

CONOVER. Well, remember we have control of the Investigating Committees. We can dig up plenty to throw at the Administration.

SPIKE. (*Crossing behind desk R. with drinks.*) Oh, if we dig it up, Wallace will do the throwing. (*He places drinks in front of* KAY *and* CONOVER. *Crosses back to table L. and starts mixing* GRANT'S *drink.*)

KAY. Jim, this is important: that veto has made Truman strong with labor. We have to make some appeal to the labor vote and that means we have to have the right candidate.

SPIKE. That rules out Westbrook Pegler.

KAY. But it doesn't rule out Grant. (*She rises and crosses to* C.) No employer in the country's got a better labor record. And business is bound to go along with him. (*Crosses back to chair L. of desk.*) Jim, don't you see the strength we have in Mr. Matthews? Phil Murray and Pegler would both vote for him.

GRANT. I'm not so sure—because I wouldn't promise either one of them anything.

SPIKE. You'd have to promise them something. (*Crosses to* GRANT *with drink, pauses for thought.*) Still, Dewey outpromised Roosevelt and it didn't get him anywhere. I would like to pause at this moment and take a one-man Gallup Poll. What do you think of Mr. Matthews' chances, Jim?

CONOVER. That's not an easy question to answer. I haven't got much to go on. After Mr. Matthews makes his speech here Monday night I'd know a little more about what the feeling is here in Washington. Is Mrs. Matthews coming down to hear you speak?

GRANT. (*Amiably.*) No, Mrs. Matthews takes bringing up the children more seriously than she does my speeches. And I think she's right. This has all been very flattering—but as I said to Mrs. Thorndyke while you were out of the room—let's drop the whole idea.

KAY. (*Quickly. To* CONOVER.) Jim, on Tuesday Grant's starting a tour of his plants. Everywhere he's going he's been invited to speak.

SPIKE. (*Crossing to L. of* KAY.) Minneapolis, Seattle, San Francisco, Los Angeles, Denver, Wichita, and Detroit.

KAY. If Grant made those speeches, at the end of the tour could you tell him whether he had a chance, or whether we should give up the whole idea?

CONOVER. That covers a lot of territory. Yes, I think if Mr. Matthews made those speeches I could be pretty definite.

KAY. (*Crossing to* GRANT.) Grant, you've got to go along with us that far. You've got to make those speeches.

GRANT. (*Looking up at* KAY.) Look.—Kay, I'm going to be pretty busy on this trip. I've got problems in every one of those plants. Besides, I wish I knew how much you had to do with those invitations for me to speak.

KAY. (*Decisively—crossing to* C.) Well, anyway, you're going to accept them. Spike, you're going to make the trip with him. You've been telling everyone for years how to run a political campaign. Now we'll find out whether you can run one. (*Crosses back to her chair* L. *of desk.*) The bureau can get along without you for a couple of weeks. It will be a vacation for you. (SPIKE *crosses to table* L.)

CONOVER. It will be a vacation for everyone in Washington. Now that we've reached that decision, there's a lot for all of us to talk about. On this tour, Mr. Matthews —— (*Phone rings.* CONOVER *reaches for it.*) Damn! (*Into phone.*) Hello. (*With some interest.*) Oh, yes, I've been waiting to hear from you. (*Looks around room unhappily.*) Hold on. Wait a minute. (*Looks at* SPIKE *and rises.*) Spike, why don't you go home? (*Hands phone to* KAY.) Do you mind, Mrs. Thorndyke?

KAY. (*Takes phone.*) I'm glad you trust publishers.

CONOVER. (*Crossing to door.*) Just Republican publishers. (KAY *crosses to front of desk.*)

SPIKE. I thought it was agreed we were all to trust each other.

CONOVER. Only when we're in the same room. (*He exits.*)

SPIKE. (*Crossing to* C. *and gleefully rubbing his hands.*) Mr. Conover has just leaped gracefully onto the front seat of the band wagon.

GRANT. Take it easy, Spike. Conover hasn't brought up the payoff yet.

SPIKE. (*Crossing to* GRANT.) Well, there's one promise I want.

GRANT. What?

SPIKE. That I'm not to be the next Postmaster General.

GRANT. I'll settle for that, Spike—you're not the next Postmaster

General. And that's the only commitment I'm going to make.

SPIKE. You settled awful quick. I just threw that in for a laugh. (*Crosses* R. C. *and addresses* KAY.) Mrs. Thorndyke—tell Sir Galahad here ——

KAY. (*Into phone.*) Are you on? All right, I'll hang up. (KAY *starts phone to its cradle, keeping her ear to the receiver. Suddenly her expression changes sharply. She presses down the disconnector with her free hand, then releases it immediately and continues to listen in, giving the men a warning gesture.* GRANT *rises indignantly and crosses to* C.)

GRANT. (*In a whisper.*) Kay! (SPIKE *stops him with a gesture.* GRANT *obviously disapproves and walks unhappily to back of chair* L., *as if he will have none of it.* SPIKE *beams in admiration at first, but as* KAY *listens in and flashes a look toward* GRANT, SPIKE *realizes it is a serious matter and his smile vanishes. Even* GRANT'S *attention is arrested. The two men stand watching* KAY. *She bangs up and crosses immediately to* GRANT, *speaking quickly and with deep concern.*)

KAY. It's a report from New York. He's had someone looking you up. They've picked up some gossip about you and me.

SPIKE. Oh—oh!

KAY. And there's been talk about Mary, too—Mary and some Major.

SPIKE. Who's Mary?

KAY. Mrs. Matthews.

SPIKE. Oh—ho!

GRANT. What Major? What's his name?

KAY. I couldn't get his name.

GRANT. What'd the name sound like? (KAY *gestures him to be quiet and raises her voice.*)

KAY. Sh-h. He'll be back in a minute. (*Crosses back to chair* L. *of desk. Sitting down and says too loudly.*) Of course, Spike, that's one way of looking at it, but you never can be sure. (SPIKE *crosses to table* L.)

GRANT. (*Sitting down, chair* L. *To himself.*) A Major! (*As* CON- OVER *enters.*)

SPIKE. (*To* GRANT.) On the other hand, if what you say is true, Mr. Matthews, that makes the migratory flamingo a very interesting bird.

CONOVER. (*Crossing down* C.) What makes the flamingo an interesting bird, Spike?

SPIKE. (*Caught short, but not very.*) Tell him what you just told us, Mr. Matthews.

GRANT. I don't think Mr. Conover's interested in the wild life of America.

CONOVER. Staying up this late is a little more wild life than I'm used to. I think we'd better call it a night. (*They are caught flat-footed by his tone of dismissal.*)

SPIKE. (*Tentatively.*) Nothing else you want to bring up, Jim?

CONOVER. Not now. (GRANT *rises.*) You may have a little trouble getting a taxi. Good night, Spike. (CONOVER *shakes hands with* SPIKE.)

SPIKE. Good night, Jim. Good night, Boss. (*Turns to* GRANT.) Grant, if the lights are still on in the White House, I'll drop in and tell the Trumans to start packing.

KAY. Spike, you'd better get off some wires accepting those speaking dates for Grant.

CONOVER. I'd like to give some of those cities a little more thought. (SPIKE *gets hat and crosses to door. To* GRANT.) Tomorrow's time enough for that, isn't it?

GRANT. Yes—I guess so. (*He crosses to* CONOVER.) Well, Mr. Conover, if I never get any closer to the White House than this, it's been a very pleasant evening. (*Crosses to* C.) I'll say good night, too.

CONOVER. You and I might take time to finish our drinks.

KAY. I haven't finished mine—(*No one asks her to stay,* CONOVER *partly turns toward her.*) I'll finish it in my room. (*She starts to rise, picking up bag and drink.* SPIKE *opens door.*)

CONOVER. (*To* KAY.) I thought Mr. Matthews and I might chat for a few minutes longer.

KAY. I'll run along, then. I can't tell you how grateful we are for your having us here. Good night. Good night, Grant.

GRANT. Good night, Kay.

KAY. (*Starts to door, stops and turns back to* CONOVER; SPIKE *is holding door open for her.*) Jim, I want you to know how completely we trust you. (*She goes directly to* GRANT.) Good night, darling. (*She puts her arms around him and they kiss. She starts out again.*)

CONOVER. Mrs. Thorndyke. (KAY *stops and turns.*) You might as well finish your drink here. That's what I was going to talk about. (KAY *raises her eyebrows, comes back and sits down.* CONOVER *crosses to* R. *of chair* R. SPIKE *closes door, drops hat on chair* U. L. C. *and stands at table* L.) Naturally, Mr. Matthews, when your name first came up as a possible candidate, I made some inquiries. It seems there's been some talk about you and Mrs. Thorndyke.

GRANT. What kind of talk?

CONOVER. (*Easily.*) I think you know what I mean when I say talk.

KAY. We wouldn't pretend to deny there's a basis for it, but it can't be very widespread.

GRANT. (*Crossing to* C.) Kay, let Mr. Conover tell us what he's heard.

CONOVER. That's about all. There's been some gossip. That's nothing unusual, and as long as it's about a man who makes airplanes, even though you're very well known I don't think it would spread a great deal, but the minute you become a public figure ——

KAY. You think it might be used against Mr. Matthews?

CONOVER. Not openly. What it would come down to would be a whispering campaign.

GRANT. Frankly, Mr. Conover, I don't give a damn for the kind of opinion that sort of thing would influence.

CONOVER. I haven't any respect for it, either; but I have to reckon with it. You see, Mr. Matthews, while Mrs. Thorndyke happens to be divorced, you're a married man.

GRANT. Well, if you think that's a major—(*His mind sticks momentarily on the word " major."*)—a vital factor . . . Kay, that seems to settle it. (*He starts to door.*)

KAY. Wait a minute, Grant! Jim, there must be some way around this ——

CONOVER. Yes, there's a very obvious one.

GRANT. (*Coming back to* C.) So? What is it?

CONOVER. I'd like to see your wife with you when you speak here Monday night; I'd like to see her make this trip with you.

GRANT. (*Laughing.*) That's not the solution. If Mary knew that I even thought of myself as President of the United States ——

KAY. No, Jim, we've got to think of something else. It's a little difficult for me to talk about Mrs. Matthews in this situation, but

15

—you've seen the kind of wife—the more important her husband becomes the more determined she is to make him feel unimportant.

GRANT. Now, wait a minute, Kay. Be fair to Mary. (*To* CONOVER.) I don't want you to get the wrong impression of my wife, Mr. Conover. She's no shrew. She's a damned bright woman.

KAY. Grant, you know Mary's always cutting you down.

GRANT. I can't deny that. Still, I suppose her criticism of me has been valuable sometimes. (*To* CONOVER.) But a man does reach a saturation point.

CONOVER. If you become a candidate you'll have to take a lot of criticism.

SPIKE. (*Crossing to* C.) Yes, your wife might be good training for you. Toughen you up.

KAY. (*To* CONOVER.) I think it's more important that Grant should have his self-confidence.

CONOVER. (*Crossing to sit on edge of desk.*) The most important thing of all is to kill this gossip. We haven't got a chance unless we do. (*Crossing to sit on edge of desk.*) The American people like to think of a married candidate as happily married. They want to see him and his wife together. They like to see them make the campaign together. It's an American tradition. You'd have to face that sooner or later. I think the sooner you face it the better.

GRANT. Yes, Mary may solve the whole situation for us. I'm not so sure she would campaign with me even if I asked her to.

CONOVER. Why don't you call her and find out? (KAY *and* GRANT *exchange looks.*)

GRANT. Why not? (CONOVER *dials phone—there is a slight pause and then* SPIKE *speaks.*)

SPIKE. There's been that gossip about every candidate except Herbert Hoover. They didn't pull it on Hoover because nobody would have believed it.

CONOVER. (*Into phone.*) This is Dupont 4108. I want a New York call. (KAY *rises and crosses upstage behind desk.*) I want to speak to Mrs. Grant Matthews at —— (*He looks inquiringly at* GRANT.)

GRANT. Plaza 5-8249.

CONOVER. (*Into phone.*) Plaza 5-8249. (*He rises and hands phone to* GRANT.) Invite her to stay here, of course.

GRANT. (*Taking phone.*) There's no way of a man being elected President before his wife hears about it, is there? (CONOVER

crosses and stands above chair R. *He sits in chair* L. *of desk.*)
Hello. Well, put it through as soon as you can and call me.
(*He hangs up and there is an uneasy pause. They are not looking
at each other. Finally* SPIKE *speaks up brightly.*)
SPIKE. Shall we dance? (CONOVER *gives him a look that's an an-
swer, but not to his question.*)
GRANT. (*Looking up at* CONOVER.) Mr. Conover, I'm glad there's
a delay in that call because before it comes through there's something I'd like to ask you.
CONOVER. Yes?
GRANT. If it works out that we can go ahead, you and I, what are
you going to expect of me?
CONOVER. I'd expect you to be elected.
GRANT. Mr. Conover, I'm inexperienced in politics, but I am not
—shall I say—completely naive. Let's put it this way—if I were
elected, naturally I'd be very grateful to you. Is there any par-
ticular way in which you'd expect me to show my gratitude?
KAY. (*Drops down to above desk.*) Grant, aren't you being a little
premature?
GRANT. It's probably pre-natal influence. I was a premature baby.
SPIKE. You were? Say, drop that into an interview sometime.
There may be some votes in that. There are a lot of people who
think they were seven-month babies.
CONOVER. In answer to your question, Mr. Matthews, if you mean
have I a list of Federal appointments in my pocket?—No.
GRANT. I'd be very glad to see any list of names you wanted to
show me. I just want it to be clear I'm not making any commitments.
CONOVER. I can ask for no more than an open mind. Mrs. Thorndyke said you two came down here for my advice. Well, politics
is my business. If we do get into a campaign together I hope
you'll be open-minded about any advice I might give you then.
GRANT. I'd welcome it—only I can't promise I'd always follow it.
KAY. (*Crossing down to* L. *of* GRANT.) Now, Grant, don't turn
down advice before you get it.
GRANT. (*To* CONOVER, *with a disarming laugh.*) All right. Give
me some!
CONOVER. (*Amused, but still serious.*) Well, in that list of speaking dates, you mentioned Minneapolis. I wouldn't speak there.

17

You might just stir up trouble. That's Stassen territory. The local boys would resent it and you might start a backfire.

GRANT. That's damn good advice. I'll take it. How do you feel about Stassen?

CONOVER. He's a little too liberal for some of the boys. There's a good deal of opposition to him in the party. Oh, that prompts me to venture some more advice, if you don't mind?

GRANT. No—shoot!

CONOVER. If you make this preliminary tour, keep whatever you have to say pretty general. Don't be too specific.

GRANT. There I'm afraid I can't go all the way with you. (KAY looks at SPIKE who starts walking upstage to behind desk.) The only reason I have for speaking at all is because there are some things I feel deeply about ——

KAY. Grant, it's only that at this early stage ——

GRANT. No, Kay! I'm not going to pull any punches! I want that understood!

KAY. Grant, if you keep on being belligerent about your honesty, we'll begin to suspect you.

CONOVER. (Serenely.) Mr. Matthews, most candidates have to spend a lot of time explaining things they wish they hadn't said, and often they have to explain it again and again and again. You're not carrying that weight because you haven't said very much yet. (He sits in chair R.)

SPIKE. Look how much Dewey can talk without saying anything.

CONOVER. Your danger at this point might be in raising minor issues that come back to plague you later. My advice to you would be to stay in the middle of the road.

GRANT. I don't know. The middle of the road's getting pretty crowded.

KAY. Grant, this isn't the airplane business. You're used to dealing with tangible things. I know what Jim Conover's talking about, because I have to go out after circulation. You'll have to go out after votes.

GRANT. Oh, I know you have to appeal for votes. But I think what I believe in —— (The phone rings. SPIKE picks it up.)

SPIKE. (Into phone.) Hello. New York? Just a minute. (He hands phone to GRANT. KAY crosses to chair L. and sits down.)

GRANT. (Into phone.) Hello. Hello. What's that? (With a little impatience.) Well, get them back. No, I'll hang on.

CONOVER. Have you your speech for Monday night prepared?

GRANT. Yes. Want to look at it tomorrow? I'll listen to anything you have to say.

KAY. And on the tour you listen to Spike. (SPIKE *crosses to* C.) He can be very valuable.

GRANT. (*Grinning.*) If I know Spike, he's going to give me plenty of advice.

SPIKE. No, Mr. Matthews, my big job is to humanize you.

GRANT. (*In amused surprise—looking up.*) Oh, is it?

SPIKE. I've got a lot of things dreamed up. Do you know what first sold Willkie to the country as a human being? Going on Information Please. He came over as a regular guy, and he held his own, too.

GRANT. Just a minute, I'm no Wendell Willkie—I'm willing to take on Harry Truman, but not John Kieran.

SPIKE. Well, we've got to do something to counteract those speeches.

GRANT. Counteract them! Well, then, why am I making them?

SPIKE. Oh, no, you've got to make them. But sometimes your speeches get a little fancy. We don't want people to think you're stuffy.

GRANT. You know, Spike, you sound just like my wife. (*Into phone.*) Hello, Mary. I'm in Washington. (*Pause.* SPIKE *crosses to table* L.) How's Joyce? (*Pause.*) Doctor been there today? (*Pause.*) That's fine . . . if she's that well Sonny won't catch it now. . . . (*Pause.*) Mary, I'm making another speech down here Monday night. (*Pause.*) No, they *asked* me to! I'd like to have you come down and listen to it, if it wouldn't bore you too much. (*Pause.*) As a matter of fact, I won't *be* home for a few weeks. I'm making a tour of the plants. How'd you like to make the trip with me?—I wish you would. We haven't made the circuit together in a long time. (*Pause.*) But how about coming down *here*, anyway? We'll be house guests at Jim Conover's. (*Pause.*) Conover—a friend of mine, but in spite of that you'll like him. (*Pause.*) Get here tomorrow night . . . it doesn't matter how late. I'll send a plane back for you. . . . Swell! (*Pause.*) Bring enough clothes for the trip, anyway. We can talk it over when you get here. (*Pause.*) Oh, and, Mary, you'll need a dinner dress here Monday night. It's a banquet. You'll get my speech for dessert. (*Pause.*) What? (*Pause.*) All right.—Of course you'll

19

look a little funny sitting there with earmuffs on. Good night. (*He
hangs up, looks at* CONOVER.) I'm not sure the presidency's worth
it.
CONOVER. She's coming?
GRANT. Yes, Heaven help me.
KAY. Grant, you know what that means. If Mary's coming here
I've got to go home tomorrow.
CONOVER. I confess that would ease the housing situation. The
National Committee seems to think I run a hotel.
KAY. (*Rising and crossing to* U. C.) Well, for the next few weeks
I'll be sitting alone in New York, while you tour the country with
your wife.
SPIKE. " Politics makes strange bedfellows." (*Curtain starts down
as* KAY *gives him a look.* SPIKE *catches the look, picks up his hat
and starts out of the room.*)

CURTAIN

ACT I

SCENE 2

TIME: *The next night.*
A bedroom in JIM CONOVER'S *house. There is a double
bed with lamps on bed tables each side of bed. There
are two or three overstuffed armchairs and the other
usual furniture. The entrance to the bedroom is* U.
stage L. *Off the bedroom,* U. R., *is a dressing-room leading to
a bathroom.*
DISCOVERED AT RISE: GRANT, *wearing horn-rimmed
glasses, is discovered alone, seated at a desk* D. R., *editing
the loose pages of his typewritten speech. There is a
knock at the door.*

GRANT. (*Taking off glasses.*) Come in! (CONOVER *enters.*)
CONOVER. How's the speech coming along?
GRANT. All right, I guess. What Spike said last night had me wor-
ried. I'm trying to unfancy it a little bit.
CONOVER. (*Crossing to* L. *of* GRANT.) Don't let Spike worry you.
I think it's very good. When you finish, drop back downstairs. I

20

think it would be a good idea to have the boys see as much of you as possible. You made a very good impression at dinner.

GRANT. I was thrown a little by the way Senator Fosdick kept yessing me. He was an America Firster, wasn't he?

CONOVER. Yes, he was—until he was defeated. (*He starts to leave.*) I'll see you later, then. (*Turns back.*) Oh! I came up to tell you I've sent the car down to the airport.

GRANT. (*Looking at his watch.*) He might have quite a wait. I don't think Mary will be in much before midnight. (*A little disturbed.*) If she could have told me when she was getting in I could have met her myself. (SPIKE *enters, closing door after him and crossing* D. C.)

SPIKE. Jim, Governor Dunn just arrived.

CONOVER. Oh, that's fine! (*To* GRANT.) I want you to meet him. He can be very valuable to you in the Northwest. I'm glad he dropped in.

SPIKE. Like hell you are! He brought his bags with him.

CONOVER. Oh, damn! Where am I going to put him? Well, I guess I'll have to take him into my room. I was hoping for a good night's sleep. (*Crosses to* SPIKE.) Spike, you're an expert in these matters. Why do all governors snore?

SPIKE. It's an occupational disease.

GRANT. Where are you putting Mary? (CONOVER *is taken a little by surprise.*)

CONOVER. (*Turning back to* GRANT.) Why, in here with you. If we're going to create the impression about you two that we want to, this would be a good start.

GRANT. (*Troubled.*) I don't think she'd welcome the idea. We rushed into this decision and it's been on my conscience ever since. Look, Jim, when Mary finds out what's up, she can still say no. But moving her in here with me tonight ——

CONOVER. (*Thinking.*) Well, Senator Fosdick's room is about the only one. He's in there alone. But where can I put the Senator? There's nothing left but the billiard table.

SPIKE. Why not? You can drop that bald head right in the corner pocket.

CONOVER. I'll put him on a cot somewhere. Come on down with me. I want you to meet the Governor. (*He crosses to door.*)

SPIKE. (*Crossing* R.) He's got to finish that speech. I want to take it with me tonight.

21

GRANT. I'm almost through.

CONOVER. (*Turning at door.*) Shall I send up a drink?

SPIKE. (*At desk.*) Send up a couple. (CONOVER *exits.*)

GRANT. Why are you in such a hurry? There's plenty of time to get this copied before tomorrow night.

SPIKE. All the wire services will want this by noon, and even if they don't want it they're going to get it. (*He crosses back of desk above* GRANT.) If they don't have it in advance you may only get a couple of paragraphs. Are you out on a limb anywhere in here? (*He picks up first few pages of manuscript and starts glancing through it.*) Because we could play it the other way. Not give out any copies—then you could always claim you've been misquoted.

GRANT. I wish I was as sure as you seem to be that I'll be quoted at all.

SPIKE. (*Crossing down to* L. *of desk.*) This isn't as bad as I thought it was going to be.

GRANT. Those changes were all made for your benefit. (GRANT *has finished last page.*)

SPIKE. (*Placing one sheet in front of* GRANT.) This spot in here sounds a little like a speech. (*He points. Crosses* L. C. *with three pages in hand.*)

GRANT. (*Turning at desk.*) Damn it!—It *is* a speech!

SPIKE. That's what I meant. (*There is a knock on the door.*)

GRANT. Come in! (NORAH *enters, loaded down with two bags and a hat-box.*)

NORAH. (*From doorway.*) These are Mrs. Matthews' bags.

GRANT. (*Rising.*) Oh, is my wife here?

NORAH. She just came. I'll put these in the dressing-room. (*She starts for dressing-room.* GRANT *stops her.*)

GRANT. No, they don't go there. Mrs. Matthews is in another room.

NORAH. (*Bewildered.*) What other room? (*Enter* CONOVER.)

CONOVER. Grant, Mrs. Matthews is here. (*He crosses to above chair* L. MARY *follows* CONOVER *in.* MARY *is an attractive woman in her thirties, dressed in a smart traveling suit and hat.*)

GRANT. (D. R. C.) Hello, dear.

MARY. (*Crossing to* GRANT. CONOVER *closes door.*) Hello, Grant. (*She and* GRANT *kiss.*)

GRANT. I didn't expect you to get here this early.

MARY. I think we broke the record—and both my ear-drums.

GRANT. Spike, I want you to meet Mrs. Matthews. (*To* MARY.) This is Mr. MacManus.

MARY. How do you do, Mr. MacManus?

SPIKE. (*Standing* L. *near window.*) Hello, Mrs. Matthews.

GRANT. You seem to have met Mr. Conover.

MARY. Oh, yes, downstairs. (*She smiles at* CONOVER, *who is standing* L. C.) It's so nice of you to have us here. (*Turns to* GRANT.) I'm really quite excited. I hope you'll notice, Grant, I've packed for the whole trip. (*She points to bags, which* NORAH *is still holding. To* NORAH.) Just put those bags down somewhere.

NORAH. I was told you were going to be in another room?

CONOVER. Leave the bags here for a minute, Norah. You're moving Senator Fosdick.

NORAH. (*Crossing* L. *toward* CONOVER.) Again?

CONOVER. Put him in the south bedroom with Mr. Godfrey.

NORAH. The Commissioner's in there with Mr. Godfrey.

CONOVER. We have another cot, haven't we?

NORAH. That army cot.

MARY. That's nonsense. Don't move Senator Fosdick. Grant and I can stay here. (*She looks around at group.*) We're really married. (CONOVER *hesitates.* MARY *looks at* GRANT.) Unless the rest of the Senate is in here with Grant.

GRANT. Mr. Conover just thought you'd be more comfortable with a room to yourself.

MARY. (*To* NORAH.) I'll stay here. (NORAH *crosses to dressing-room.* GRANT *crosses up to hold door open for her.* MARY *goes to* L. *of bed and throws hat and bag on it. She starts removing her gloves.*) After all, Senator Fosdick's an Isolationist. I think he ought to be isolated.

SPIKE. (*Grinning.*) I'm going to like you. (MARY *answers him with a smile.*)

NORAH. (*At dressing-room door,* U. R.) Shall I unpack for you, Ma'am?

MARY. Just the small bag. And you can take the shoes out of my hat-box. (NORAH *starts out.*) Oh, there's a print dress in the suitcase I'd like to wear tomorrow. Could it be pressed for me?

NORAH. Surely. (*She exits into dressing-room with bags.*)

MARY. (*Pressing her ears.*) These plane trips always leave me deaf.

GRANT. (*Crossing* D. R.) If that lasts through tomorrow you'll be spared hearing my speech. (STEVENS, *the butler, arrives with two drinks on a tray. He's a bit bewildered to find four people.*)
MARY. (*Smiling at* GRANT.) That's a little more than I could hope for. (*The others are politely amused.*)
STEVENS. (L. *of* MARY.) Scotch and soda?
MARY. Oh, I'm not as deaf as I thought I was. What a perfect host! (*She turns and takes one of the highballs.*)
CONOVER. I'll take that, Stevens. (*He crosses to* STEVENS *and takes other drink. To* GRANT.) Grant, you and Spike get your drinks downstairs. I want you to meet the Governor. (STEVENS *exits.*)
GRANT. Want to meet a Governor, Mary?
MARY. I'd like to get a little better acquainted with this highball.
CONOVER. (*To* MARY.) That was my idea. You and I, let's finish our drinks quietly up here. (*To* GRANT.) We'll join you later.
SPIKE. (*Crossing to* C.) How about the rest of this Gettysburg Address? Finished with it?
GRANT. (*Crossing to desk to get papers.*) Yes, I think the end's all right. Take it along. (*Crosses* C. *to* SPIKE *and hands him papers.*)
CONOVER. Spike, see that Grant and Governor Dunn get together. (SPIKE *crosses to door,* GRANT *following him.*)
SPIKE. (*Exiting.*) Right.
CONOVER. I'm sure the Governor will be very interested in meeting you, Grant.
GRANT. (*At door, with a touch of self-importance.*) I'll be glad to talk to him. (GRANT *exits.* MARY *smiles at* CONOVER *and crosses to chair* R. *of table* L. C.)
MARY. Oh, this is very pleasant. (*She sits down.*)
CONOVER. It is for me.
MARY. Now I can boast that I've really been behind the scenes in Washington.
CONOVER. (*Standing* R. *of her chair.*) You certainly can! The Republican party's been behind the scenes for fifteen years. However, that's over. We've got Congress and in '48 we'll have the White House.
MARY. If I needed an excuse to drink, that would be it. (*She lifts her glass to* CONOVER. *He lifts his.*) But giving the country a change isn't good enough. We've got to give them a change for the better.

24

CONOVER. Your husband's been lecturing me along those lines.

MARY. Then I'd better change the subject. Grant can be very outspoken—but not by anybody I know. (*She takes a drink.*)

CONOVER. Everything he said about politicians we had coming to us. Mrs. Matthews, I have a great admiration for your husband. (*He crosses to chair L.*)

MARY. (*Turning in chair to face CONOVER.*) I'm many years ahead of you on that.

CONOVER. Of course, everyone admires him as a business man. What impresses me is that he doesn't limit his thinking to his own field. (CONOVER *sits down.*) He has a very clear vision about the whole country—what it needs—what the world needs. Any man who sees our problems as clearly as he does—it imposes on him a certain responsibility.

MARY. Oh, I think you're sure of a big check from him. (*She takes another swallow of drink.* CONOVER *smiles, then becomes serious.*)

CONOVER. No, I mean a responsibility to the country. I've been trying to persuade your husband to take an active part in the government.

MARY. Mr. Conover, Grant's talking politics is one thing—but he has a big enough job ahead of him—that is, if you know anything about his plans for world aviation.

CONOVER. I don't think his usefulness should be limited to that. I think the country will feel that way, too, after hearing what he says here Monday night, and the speeches he's going to make on this trip.

MARY. Is he going to make speeches on the trip?

CONOVER. Yes, in several places.

MARY. (*Dismayed.*) Oh, dear. (*Catching herself.*) Oh, I didn't mean that the way it sounded. Grant really can make a very good speech. But public appearances for me—I'm not good at that—I'm so uncomfortable. Would it be bad form if I just stayed quietly at the hotel and listened to him over the radio?

CONOVER. Yes, I'm afraid it would. It would defeat the whole purpose.

MARY. Purpose? What purpose?

CONOVER. Mrs. Matthews, you must know how concerned your husband is about this country's splitting apart—how deeply he feels that it must be held together.

25

MARY. Oh, yes. We've been talking about it for months. Grant's been trying to figure out what could be done.

CONOVER. I think you can help him do something about it.

MARY. No, not me. I just get angry! I can't read the newspapers any more! While the war was on we were a united country—we were fighting Germany and Japan. Now we're just fighting each other. No, I just get angry. (*Takes drink.*)

CONOVER. I'm glad you feel that strongly about it, because it's important that wherever Grant goes now—wherever he makes these speeches—you're right there alongside of him.

MARY. Why should that be important?

CONOVER. Well, for a man who's going to be in the public eye—people like to know his wife—like to see what she looks like—like to see the two of them together.

MARY. (*Thoughtfully, putting drink on table.*) Oh! I see. I was a little puzzled by Grant's invitation to make this trip with him.

CONOVER. Oh, Grant wants you to go along. These public appearances—they're my idea. It's just an old politician's habit of cashing in on an opportunity.

MARY. (*Rising and making turn behind chair L. C.*) It all fits in a little too neatly, Mr. Conover. I don't know whether you know— (*She stops and looks at him sharply.*)—or perhaps you do—that Grant and I haven't been very close for the last year or so!

CONOVER. Wouldn't you prefer to create a contrary impression?

MARY. (*Back of chair L. C.*) Oh, then you do know! Let's be open about this. These public appearances that Grant and I are to make together—are they designed to kill off any talk about my husband and Mrs. Thorndyke?

CONOVER. (*Putting his drink on table.*) There's that kind of talk about every important man. But if there are any rumors about your husband, this would be a good chance to kill them. (*CONOVER is watching MARY carefully.*) You see, Mrs. Matthews —— (*NORAH enters from dressing-room, carrying a print dress. She crosses to C. and stops.*)

NORAH. Is this the dress, Ma'am? (*MARY stares at dress and then comes to the surface.*)

MARY. Oh, yes. But don't bother to press it. (*She crosses below NORAH to R. C.*)

NORAH. (*Crossing to door U. L.*) It's no trouble at all, Ma'am. It won't take me long. I'll have it back tonight. (*NORAH exits.*)

26

MARY. (*Turns and crosses to door* U. L.) No! Please! (*She turns and looks around room to locate phone, then to* CONOVER.) May I use your telephone?

CONOVER. Certainly.

MARY. (*Crossing to phone on table* L. *of bed.*) I want to get back to New York tonight if I can. (*She picks up receiver.*)

CONOVER. (*Rising.*) Mrs. Matthews, I think any man who has a chance to become President of the United States deserves that chance. (MARY *stares at him in astonishment. Puts down receiver and crosses slowly to chair* L. C., *staring at* CONOVER *during cross.*)

MARY. President of the United States?

CONOVER. Yes. (*There is a short pause.*) Don't you think he'd make a good President?

MARY. (*After consideration.*) Yes, I do.

CONOVER. Then you understand this goes beyond personal considerations. Let's not think of this in terms of you—and Grant ——

MARY. —and Mrs. Thorndyke.

CONOVER. And Mrs. Thorndyke. I'm sure you will go along with us. You're a good citizen.

MARY. Right now, Mr. Conover, I'm not feeling like a good citizen! I'm feeling like a woman!

CONOVER. All right, as a woman!

MARY. As a woman, no, I won't go along with you. (*She crosses to* R. C.) I resent being used!

CONOVER. Mrs. Matthews, let's think of it in terms of the country. That's what I've had to do. (*He crosses to* C.) I am prepared to make some sacrifices.

MARY. (*Turning to him.*) What sacrifices?

CONOVER. Frankly, your husband isn't the kind of man a politician would prefer to deal with.

MARY. I've been wondering why any political party should choose Grant, knowing the things he stands for.

CONOVER. I want the people to make the choice.

MARY. (*Angrily.*) That's awfully big of you!

CONOVER. That's the purpose of this trip. I want the American people to get better acquainted with your husband. We don't know yet what's coming out of it, but I've told him that when this trip is over I can let him know whether to go ahead with the idea, or forget the whole thing.

27

MARY. Oh, I don't think Grant could ever forget it. I'll bet he's running a pretty high fever right now. When he left the room I thought he walked as though he was trying to be two inches taller.

CONOVER. Mrs. Matthews, you see your husband at pretty close range. Take my word for it, he's a big man.

MARY. There's no argument about that, Mr. Conover. I know he's a big man and you know he's a big man. My bad days are when *he* knows he's a big man! (*Crosses upstage between door and bed R. Thinks a moment.*) You don't suppose there's any way of Grant being elected President and keeping it a secret from him, do you? (CONOVER *laughs.* MARY *sits on* R. *side of bed.*) Is Grant speaking in Seattle?

CONOVER. Yes, why?

MARY. We were married in Seattle. When I think of Grant speaking there as a candidate for President ——

CONOVER. (*Crossing to* R. *of* MARY.) He's not speaking now as a candidate. That's a deep, dark secret. The whole idea of this trip is to create the demand.

MARY. Oh, that clears up something you just said—he's your choice first and then the people's choice.

CONOVER. (*Amused.*) I'm a citizen. I have a right to a choice. I want to help Grant all I can. He's new at this and needs some advice.

MARY. What advice are you giving him?

CONOVER. Oh, so far it's chiefly along the lines of what not to say. Your husband is so afraid of not being completely honest.

MARY. You want him to be honest, don't you?

CONOVER. Oh, yes! (*There is a knock on the door.*) Yes? Come in! (STEVENS *enters.*)

STEVENS. There's a long distance call for you, sir. It's Mr. Treadwell.

CONOVER. Thank you, Stevens. (*Crosses to* C., *turns and looks at* MARY.) I'll take it here. (CONOVER *goes to phone.* STEVENS *exits.*)

MARY. Am I in the way?

CONOVER. Not at all. I won't be a minute. (*He picks up phone.*) Hello. Put him on. (*Pause.*) Yes. How are you? (*Pause.*) Uh-huh. Yes, Joe, I'm sorry, too. We should have carried that county. You'll have to change your whole campaign for '48. You'll have to find some other issues. How many Italians down there? (*Pause.*)

What's the size of your Polish vote? (*Pause.*) That many? Tell them their hope lies in our Party. We'll really get tough with Russia. We'll force her to correct those injustices. (*Pause—*MARY *turns and looks at* CONOVER.) You don't have to tell 'em how. Go after it hammer and tongs. (MARY *rises and crosses* D. S.) You show me you can swing that county in '48 and I'll get you that Veterans' Hospital. Not at all. Good luck and thanks for calling. (CONOVER *hangs up and drops* D. S.) I'm sorry for the interruption.

MARY. I'm glad it happened. (*Crossing to* CONOVER.) It gave me a chance to change my mind. I'll go with Grant.

CONOVER. (*Heartily.*) That's fine! That pleases me very much. That's our first big campaign contribution. (*Raises glass.*) To you, my dear, the most attractive plank in your husband's platform.

MARY. That's a hell of a thing to call a woman.

CONOVER. (*Laughing, putting glass on table.*) Suppose we go downstairs? I'd like you to meet the rest of my guests. (*Makes motion toward door.*)

MARY. (*Crossing* L. *a little.*) Would it be rude if I postponed that until tomorrow? I have to get a little used to this idea—and I have to get a little used to Grant.

CONOVER. Well, this trip—working along with Grant—by the time you come back, you two may be much closer together.

MARY. Even if that could happen, I don't think you'd want it to. It might cost you the support of Mrs. Thorndyke's newspapers.

CONOVER. (*Laughing.*) Don't worry about that. They're Republican newspapers in Republican territory. They couldn't afford to risk their circulation. A chain of newspapers is a very valuable property.

MARY. Mrs. Thorndyke must have thought so. In the divorce settlement Dick Thorndyke got the children and she got the newspapers. (*Crosses to* L. C. *and turns.*) And if that sounds bitchy, I hoped it would. (*Crosses far* L. *and then back* R. *back of chairs.*) You may succeed in killing the rumors, but unfortunately you won't kill Mrs. Thorndyke.

CONOVER. (*Knowingly.*) We may kill more than one rumor.

MARY. Oh, dear! Is there someone I don't know about?

CONOVER. (*With a smile.*) There have been some rumors about you.

MARY. (*Enormously pleased, crossing to* CONOVER.) There have?

CONOVER. Yes. About you and a certain Major.

MARY. That's wonderful! That's the best news I've had in weeks. (*Crosses* R. C. *and then turns back to* CONOVER.) Does Grant know about the Major?

CONOVER. Not so far as I know.

MARY. Well, you're going to tell him, aren't you? I deserve some· thing out of this! I was hoping he'd told *you.*

CONOVER. No, Mrs. Matthews, I have a little intelligence service of my own.

MARY. Well, it can't be too intelligent. They're considerably be· hind the times. The Major's been in Japan for six months. But when you tell Grant about him, don't let him know the Major's out of the country.

CONOVER. As far as I'm concerned, the whole thing's a military secret.

MARY. (*Gaily.*) You know, I think I'll go downstairs with you at that! I feel a lot better than I did! Can you wait until I put on a new face? (*She crosses to* R. *of bed to get her bag. The door opens and* GRANT *enters. To* GRANT.) We were just starting down.

GRANT. (*Crossing down* C.) You're a little late. The party's break· ing up.

CONOVER. (*Turning to* MARY.) We forgot all about you. We've been having a very interesting talk.

GRANT. That puts you one up on me. I've been listening to Gov· ernor Dunn. He's just about talked himself to sleep.

CONOVER. (*Concerned.*) I'd better get back down there! He doesn't even know where his room is! (*To* MARY.) I'm the night clerk around here. I'll make your excuses, Mrs. Matthews.

MARY. Thanks. Thanks for everything!

CONOVER. Good night. Good night, Grant. (*He starts for door.*)

GRANT. See you in the morning. (*He crosses up to* R. *of door.*)

CONOVER. (*At door.*) Grant, I couldn't wait. I told Mrs. Mat· thews all about it. (*He gives* GRANT *a reassuring smile and exits quickly.* GRANT *turns and looks at* MARY. *He seems a little uncer· tain. There is a pause.*)

MARY. (*Right foot of bed.*) Grant, I'm very proud of you.

GRANT. Well, Mary, it's a pretty slim chance. Don't think I'm tak· ing this too seriously. (*He comes down to* L. *of bed.*)

MARY. I'm taking it seriously. (GRANT *gives her a quick look.*) I think it would be a wonderful thing for the country.

GRANT. That's about as nice a thing as you could say, Mary. It's a damn big job. I'm not so sure I've got what it takes.

MARY. Well, I am. It isn't only that you have the brains for it.— The important thing to me is, Grant—you've always tried to be honest.

GRANT. Tried to be?

MARY. Oh, you've cut some corners in business to get where you wanted to. That's what frightens me a little. I will say this—you always had the decency to be unhappy about it.

GRANT. With some help from you.

MARY. But when you weren't thinking of yourself—when it came to what was best for the airplane industry as a whole, I've seen you take some pretty big losses.

GRANT. Right now I'm thinking about the country as a whole. I'm scared, Mary.

MARY. About being President?

GRANT. (Crossing L.) No, about what's happening to the country. It's breaking up again. . . .

MARY. What do you think you can do about it?

GRANT. I think somebody can appeal to what's best in people instead of what's worst.

MARY. And still be in politics?

GRANT. (Crossing back to L. of bed.) That's my whole case, Mary. If I can make the people see the choice they've got to make—the choice between their own interests and the interests of the country as a whole—damn it, I think the American people are sound. I think they can be unselfish.

MARY. All of them?

GRANT. (Sitting L. side of bed.) Hell, we both know there are plenty of people who'll always be out for themselves. But that's where I differ from Conover. I think they're in the minority.

MARY. I do, too. (A pause. MARY seats herself R. side of bed.) How much do you and Conover differ?

GRANT. He's a politician. (Faces front again.) Politicians think you have to bribe people to vote for you—one way or another.

MARY. You mean groups like the Poles and the Italians?

GRANT. (Turning to MARY again.) Yes—and labor and the farmers and the rest of them. But I'm not going to play politics.

MARY. That will take a lot of courage.

GRANT. No, it won't. I have faith in the American people.

31

MARY. So have I. (*A pause.*) Grant, the Presidency's a great temptation.

GRANT. I don't even want the job. Whether I become President or not is completely unimportant. (*There is a longer pause.*)

MARY. Grant, when I first learned the purpose of this trip, I wasn't very happy at the idea of making it with you.

GRANT. I can understand that.

MARY. But I am now.

GRANT. (*Looking at* MARY.) Mary, there are some things I should say—(*Pause, and he turns away.*)—but I can't. (*The moment is almost too intense.* MARY *stares at* GRANT's *back for a moment or two, then rises, taking up her hat and gloves and bag from bed.*)

MARY. Well, I think I'll get out of these clothes. (*She exits into dressing-room, leaving door open.* GRANT *rises and turns to watch door for a moment. He crosses to front of chair* L. C., *and turns to look at dressing-room door again as* MARY *speaks. Off.*) Grant!

GRANT. Yes?

MARY. (*Off.*) I wish you'd call up Joyce tomorrow.

GRANT. (*Sitting in chair* L. C.) She'll be in school, won't she?

MARY. (*Off.*) No, the doctor thinks she shouldn't go back until Wednesday. Oh, she's better. She had no temperature at all today.

GRANT. I'll call around dinner-time. Then I can talk to Sonny, too.

MARY. (*Off.*) They were both pretty disappointed they couldn't go along.

GRANT. We ought to be thinking about a good boarding school for those kids.

MARY. (*Off.*) For heaven's sake, why?

GRANT. Well, I'm not so sure the White House is a good place to raise children.

MARY. (*Off.*) Grant!

GRANT. Yes?

MARY. (*Off.*) When are you going to break the news?

GRANT. You mean that I'm a candidate?

MARY. (*Off.*) Oh, you're way beyond the nomination—you've elected yourself.

GRANT. (*Grinning.*) I walked into that one—(*Then, defensively.*) —but I didn't mean it quite the way it sounded.

MARY. (*Off.*) Which one of the plants are we going to first?

GRANT. Minneapolis.

MARY. (*Off.*) What are you speaking about there?

32

GRANT. I'm not making a speech there. That's Stassen territory. Conover thought I might just stir up trouble.

MARY. (Off.) Uh-huh. I suppose that's good politics. Tell me some more about your differences with Conover.

GRANT. (Irritated.) Now wait a minute, Mary! (Rises and crosses to dressing-room door.) That was my decision! I'm making all the decisions! I've told Conover where I stand and he knows I'm going to tell the American people where I stand. (Starts walking around to L. C.) The American people are facing problems today that will affect the future of the entire world. There's only one way to face them—with complete honesty—with utter frankness ——

MARY. (Off.) Grant!

GRANT. What?

MARY. (Off.) Take it easy. I'm going to vote for you.

GRANT. (Crossing up to L. of bed.) No, I want to straighten you out on this, too! If I have anything to offer, it's to change the whole complexion of political campaigns. I'm not going before the American people telling them what I can do for them. (Crosses down to front of chair L. C. MARY enters in nightgown, negligee and mules, and crosses to foot of bed, R.) But what I can do for them is to show them that the strength of this country, within our own borders ——

MARY. Grant! I'm through with the dressing-room.

GRANT. I'm in no hurry. The power of this country, outside our own borders ——

MARY. Wouldn't you feel more comfortable if you took off that stuffed shirt? (GRANT throws himself down in chair L. C.)

GRANT. Aw, Hell—I don't want to be President!

MARY. (Crossing to GRANT.) Darling, when we were talking a little while ago, you said the same things and they sounded so right —I wish you could just talk to the people that way.

GRANT. (Not entirely mollified.) That's the way I plan to talk to them.

MARY. That's all I meant. Got a cigarette? (GRANT offers her one from his case and lights it for her.) Bill and Amy know we're coming to Seattle?

GRANT. Bill knows—he expects me at the plant. But they don't know you're coming.

33

MARY. I'll wire Amy. (*She crosses to bench at foot of bed and sits.*) Amy—with eight children!

GRANT. Yep, Bill's got the best production record of anyone in the industry.

MARY. I hope Amy's done something about the way she dresses. She always looks as though somebody bet her she couldn't.

GRANT. (*Laughing. Turning in chair toward* MARY.) Do you remember the way she looked as your bridesmaid?

MARY. No. I was in a complete daze until we got to Victoria.

GRANT. And even in Victoria! (*Throws leg over* R. *arm of chair.*) When we went into the dining-room you shook hands with the head-waiter! (*They both laugh. There is an embarrassed pause.* GRANT *sneaks a look at* MARY, *who is sneaking a look at him at the same time.* GRANT *turns front—another look at* MARY—*then he rises and starts for the dressing-room, unbuttoning his coat, and exits, leaving door open.*) Well, I've got a tough day tomorrow. (MARY *goes back into her memories for a moment, then throws it off and crosses above for her drink on table* L. *There is a knock on the door and* MARY *goes and opens it.* NORAH *enters with* MARY'S *dress, pressed.*)

NORAH. I was afraid you might have gone to bed. I'll hang it up for you. (NORAH *starts for the dressing-room.*)

MARY. (*Crossing in front of* NORAH *and running to dressing-room door.*) My husband's in there!

NORAH. Oh.

GRANT. (*Off.*) Did you say something, darling?

MARY. No, dear. It's just the maid with my dress. (*She closes dressing-room door.* NORAH *drapes the dress carefully over back of chair* L. *of table* L., *then closes door.* MARY *comes downstage* R., *still with drink in hand, and sits at desk.*) What's your name?

NORAH. Norah, Ma'am. (*She takes extra blanket from foot of bed and puts it on back of chair* R. *of table* L.)

MARY. Thank you for pressing it, Norah. I'll hang it up later.

NORAH. (*Going to* L. *of bed and folding back spread.*) I'm sorry I was so late with it. Just as the iron got hot we got another guest.

MARY. Gracious, where did you put him?

NORAH. He's on a cot in Mr. Conover's room.

MARY. Oh, dear, that makes me feel very guilty.

NORAH. Don't you worry, Mrs. Matthews. (*She crosses to* R. *side of bed.*) A cot's good enough for most of them. They just

34

come down here to get something out of Mr. Conover. (*Turns back blanket and sheet* R. *side of bed. Starts to walk around bed to* L. *side.*) Not the people we put in this room. This room is for special guests. (*Turns back sheet and blanket on* L. *side of bed.*) We even had a Democrat in this bed one night.

MARY. Oh, I wish you hadn't told me that.

NORAH. He wasn't a Roosevelt Democrat. (NORAH *has finished with bed and turns on light on table* L. *of bed, then turns to service bell pull.*) When you wake up in the morning just press that button and I'll have breakfast right up for you. And here is the light switch here. (*She points to light switch,* R. *of door* U. L.)

MARY. Thank you, Norah. Good night.

NORAH. Good night, Ma'am. (*She starts out, then stops and turns.*) Oh, I was going to ask your husband, but maybe you can tell me. (*Crosses down* R. C.) Do you know Mrs. Thorndyke's address?

MARY. Mrs. Thorndyke?

NORAH. She forgot her glasses when she left this morning. And I know what it is to be without glasses. I want to mail them back to her.

MARY. Are you sure they're Mrs. Thorndyke's?

NORAH. (*Getting glasses from pocket and showing them.*) Yes, they're them Chinese kind. What women won't do! Won't they?

MARY. Yes—won't they? (MARY *places her drink on desk with considerable emphasis, goes to dressing-room door and opens it, calling in to* GRANT.) Grant, can you step out for a minute? Norah wants some information.

GRANT. (*Off.*) Be right with you. (MARY *crosses* L., *head high, and looks out the window, standing immovable.* GRANT *appears, tying his dressing-gown over pajamas—heartily.*) Hello, Norah. What can I do for you?

NORAH. Mrs. Thorndyke left her glasses. I wanted to know where to mail them back to her.

GRANT. Oh!—(*Glances toward* MARY.)—1276 Park Avenue. Shall I write it down for you?

NORAH. No, I can remember it. 1276. 76—that's the year of the Revolution, and twelve—for the Twelve Commandments. (NORAH *exits.* GRANT *glances toward* MARY, *who pushes window up.* GRANT *then goes back to dressing-room, closing door.* MARY *hears door close and turns. She stands for a moment in thought, staring*

35

around room, then looks first at bed and then at the overstuffed chairs. She goes into action. First she throws the pressed dress into a corner, then takes back and cushion of chair far L. and lines them up on floor up and down, stage R. of two chairs, to form part of a mattress. Next she takes seat cushion from the other chair, adding it to the two on the floor. Crossing to bed she rips blanket and top sheet off it and spreads them over mattress arrangement on floor, blanket down. She takes extra blanket from chair back to bed, pulls down sheet to bottom of bed, spreads blanket over mattress and pulls sheet up over blanket. She folds blanket and sheet double. Then taking a pillow she crosses to bed on floor. She takes off her dressing-gown and throws it on chair U. C. on top of the folded spread, then turns her attention to the bed on floor, pulling half the blanket and sheet over cushions and folding them back. As she is fixing this bed GRANT enters from dressing-room in pajamas and dressing-gown. His first glance takes in what she is up to. MARY continues working through his speech, ignoring him.)
GRANT. *(Down R. C.)* Mary, what do you think you're doing? Now stop that nonsense and make up that bed again. *(MARY continues fixing bed on floor.)* Damn it, I'm not going to let you do this! *(GRANT crosses up between floor bed and bed R. MARY has finished and turns back to light switch and turns off lights.)* You wouldn't get any sleep down there on the floor and I wouldn't get any sleep lying there—*(He points to regular bed.)*—worrying about you! *(MARY crosses quickly to bed, above GRANT, then turns to him.)*
MARY. Good night, Mr. President! *(She sits on bed, puts out lamp [BLACKOUT]. In the moonlight we see her swing into bed, pulling blankets over her—as GRANT turns and looks at bed on floor. The BLACKOUT and curtain are simultaneous.)*

CURTAIN

ACT II

SCENE: The living-room of a suite at the Book-Cadillac Hotel in Detroit. It is furnished the way a living-room in the Book-Cadillac would be furnished. The entrance from the hall is upstage C. Down R. and down L. are the two doors leading into the bedrooms of the suite.

DISCOVERED: At rise the stage is in semi-darkness, then the door to the hall opens and a BELLBOY enters with two bags, and switches on lights.

BELLBOY. Well, we made it. (*He picks up third bag and enters to* L. MARY *and* GRANT *follow him, arm-in-arm.* GRANT *is carrying a handful of telegrams, some of them already opened.*)

GRANT. Thanks! That was slick. We'd have never got through that crowd in the lobby.

BELLBOY. Remember that if you get trapped again. The service elevators are right back of the passenger elevators.

MARY. (*Crossing to* L. C.) It was exciting, wasn't it? At the station, too. What a mob!

GRANT. I thought Spike would meet us. I guess he didn't get my telegram.

MARY. Just the same I'm glad he came on ahead. This is more like it. (*Crossing to bedroom door* L.)

BELLBOY. Where shall I put the bags?

GRANT. Mary, pick a room for yourself, will you? (GRANT *throws his coat and hat on a chair in front of desk, goes to* L. *end of desk and sits on it, puts down telegrams and picks up phone.* MARY *opens door of* L. *bedroom and looks in. Into phone.*) Hello, what room is Mr. MacManus in?

MARY. That's a nice room. (*She crosses and opens door to* R. *bedroom.*)

GRANT. What? (*Pause.*) E. J. MacManus. (*Pause.*) Ring it, will you?

MARY. (*Looking into* R. *bedroom.*) One room's as good as another. (*She turns to* BELLBOY.) Where are Mr. Matthews' bags?

BELLBOY. I'll bring them right up.

37

MARY. Well, you can put those bags in here. (*She exits into* R. *bedroom, followed by* BELLBOY *with bags.*)

GRANT. (*Into phone.*) Hello, Spike. (*Pause.*) Just this minute. (*Pause.*) We were grounded in Springfield. (*Pause.*) Come on up. We're in 2519. (*Pause.*) Jim? The hell he is! Telephone the desk and tell them when he gets here to send him right up to the suite. (*Pause.*) We're having a drink. What will you have, an old-fashioned? (*Pause.*) Right. I'll order a drink for Jim, too. Come on up. (*He clicks receiver, staying on phone.*) Room service. (*Pause.*) Room service? This is 2519. Will you send up two martinis— (MARY *enters from* R. *bedroom.*) —one old-fashioned, and a Scotch and soda right away? Thanks.

MARY. Who are all the drinks for? (*She crosses to* R. *of desk.*)

GRANT. (*Picking up telegrams.*) Spike and Jim.

MARY. Is Conover here?

GRANT. He's on his way up from the station. That's a good sign, Mary. It looks as though Jim's afraid somebody might get his front seat on the bandwagon. (*Handing* MARY *batch of opened telegrams.*) Here! Let's get to work on these telegrams. (*He crosses* L. *to couch and sits at* R. *end.*)

MARY. I'm not so sure that's the reason Jim came out here.

GRANT. (*Absorbed in telegrams.*) Yeah?

MARY. (*Crossing to* R. *of* GRANT.) Grant, don't talk to Jim about what you're going to say tonight.

GRANT. (*Excitedly.*) These wires are all about the speech in Wichita. They're terrific. I've never had anything like this before.

MARY. That's what I mean. Spike tried to talk you out of making that speech. So remember what I just said.

GRANT. (*Looking up.*) What'd you just say?

MARY. Don't talk to Jim about your speech tonight.

GRANT. O. K. Mary, listen to this one. . . . (BELLBOY *enters from bedroom.*)

BELLBOY. (*Crossing to* U. C.) I turned on the radiator and opened the windows. You've got plenty of towels. Is there anything else I can do?

MARY. Yes, you can get the other bags.

BELLBOY. Oh, yes. Coming right up. (BELLBOY *exits, closing door after him.*)

MARY. Grant—these are simply wonderful! You see, you didn't

38

have to be afraid of shooting the works. That's the way they want to hear you talk.

GRANT. (*Showing* MARY *a telegram.*) Just look at these, Mary—it shows how hungry the American people are for leadership.

MARY. (*Reading a telegram.*) This one's nice, Grant. It mentions your modesty and humility. (*She gives him a sly look.*)

GRANT. Well, here's one who didn't like it.

MARY. Who's that?

GRANT. I don't know. Executive Secretary, Local 801. . . . (*He crumples wire and throws it on* L. *of sofa.*)

MARY. (*Reading another telegram.*) Look, darling—they want you to speak in Omaha next Monday.

GRANT. That's nothing. (*Pointing to pile of telegrams.*) They want me in New Orleans on Thursday and Atlanta on Friday.

MARY. Let's go—(*She crosses to sit on couch* L. *of* GRANT.)— let's go to all three of them!

GRANT. Mary, Omaha is way back there—(*He gestures.*)—New Orleans and Atlanta are way down there—(*He gestures.*)—New York is over there—(*Another gesture.*)—and the work on my desk is up to here. (*He indicates his chin.*)

MARY. I don't know why you bother with business when this is so much fun. (*They grin at each other.*)

GRANT. Do you know, this trip has done you a lot of good? You have no right to look that young at your age! (MARY *gestures, warning finger to lips.*) On the field at Denver, just before we took off, I had the damnedest sensation. You were standing there in the moonlight with the wind from the propeller blowing your hair and dress—I knew we were in Denver, but you were the girl standing on the deck of the boat on our way to Victoria.

MARY. (*After a reminiscent pause.*) Now I'll tell you something. Remember in Victoria when we stood on the balcony of the hotel, and you were telling me what the world should be like? That same boy was standing on the platform last night at Wichita.

GRANT. I'm glad you said that, Mary. It was a wonderful satisfaction, that speech—just saying what I really believed. (*Pause as they strain toward each other. Then ——*)

MARY. (*Gesturing with telegrams.*) Well, you see what that speech did! (*She looks down at a wire.*) Grant, who's Herbert Bayard Swope? *

* Change name, depending on place play is used.

39

GRANT. Oh, Mary, you know —— (*There is a knock on the door.*)
Come in! (SPIKE *enters, carrying Detroit newspapers.*) Hello,
Spike.

SPIKE. Hi-ya.

MARY. Hello, Spike, we finally got here. (*She starts picking up
telegrams from couch.*)

SPIKE. (*Closing door and coming* D. C.) You had me worried. You
jammed up a lot of appointments when your plane was grounded.

MARY. (*Crossing to* L. *of desk.*) Don't tell Grant I said so—but
there's nothing like a train.

GRANT. Those the evening papers? (*He takes papers from* SPIKE
and starts reading them, crossing to L. C.) H'mm! Front-page
spread!

SPIKE. Did the newspaper boys get you at the station?

GRANT. Yeah—a flock of them. (*He is still reading paper.*) Mary!
(MARY *gives him her attention. He reads the prominent national
headline of the current day, then sits in chair* L.)

SPIKE. Jim's coming out here makes things look pretty hot.

MARY. Is he staying here?

SPIKE. Yes, damn it—and I have to split my bed with him. You
know what kind of split a politician takes.

MARY. That's silly. We have two bedrooms here and we don't
need both of them. Grant, you're moving in with me. We're putting Jim in the other bedroom. (GRANT *is absorbed in the paper.*)
Grant! Yoo-hoo! Mr. Candidate! Mr. President!

GRANT. (*Looking up.*) Huh?

MARY. (*Snapping fingers.*) That got him! (*She crosses to* GRANT.)
I'm playing a little politics for you. I'm saving Jim from sleeping
with Spike. We're putting him in our extra bedroom.

GRANT. Fine! Be with you in a minute, Spike. Let me finish this
editorial. (*Knock on door.*)

SPIKE. I've got some people coming to see you, but they're not
due this early. (SPIKE *crosses to door and opens it.* CONOVER *enters.*) Hello, Jim!

CONOVER. Hello, Spike. (*Crosses to* MARY L. C.) Mary!

MARY. (*Crossing to* CONOVER *and embracing him.*) So nice seeing
you, Jim. We didn't expect you. (GRANT *rises.*)

CONOVER. (*Crossing to* GRANT *and shaking hands.*) Hello, Grant!
Politics agrees with you—you're looking fine.

GRANT. I feel great. Look, headlines and a damn good editorial!

It's about the Wichita speech—the responsibility of the Labor Unions.

MARY. Jim, it was the best speech Grant ever made. It was the first time I felt sure he could be elected. You never heard such applause.

CONOVER. Mary, if applause elected Presidents, William Jennings Bryan would have had three terms.

GRANT. It's good to see you, Jim.

MARY. We're putting you in our other bedroom.

CONOVER. Fine! My bags are down in the lobby.

GRANT. What news have you brought us? I'm certainly glad you're here.

MARY. Yes, it will give you a chance to see Grant in front of an audience.

CONOVER. Oh, I'm not making any public appearances. I'm not supposed to be in Detroit. Don't let anyone know I'm in town. I thought I should come out and bring you up-to-date on things and go over the situation. What are you talking about here tonight?

GRANT. Well, it's the last speech of the tour, Jim. It's got a little bit of everything. (GRANT *throws newspaper on couch.*)

CONOVER. Anything controversial?

MARY. Not for anybody that agrees with him. I want you to see these telegrams. (MARY *crosses to desk.*)

SPIKE. (*Crossing* L. *to* CONOVER.) They got here three hours late. (*To* GRANT.) I was pretty sure you'd make the broadcast. You don't go on until after the banquet.

MARY. Is this another banquet?

SPIKE. Yeah.

MARY. Then we'd better have dinner here. (MARY *picks up phone. Into phone, while waving telegrams at* SPIKE, *who crosses* R. *and gets them.* GRANT *sits with other newspaper.* CONOVER *puts hat and coat on* L. *end of sofa.*) Room service, please. What do you want to eat, Grant? (SPIKE *crosses* L. *and hands telegrams to* CONOVER.)

GRANT. Anything that's ready—hamburger if they've got it.

SPIKE. I won't have time to eat with you. Better make it snappy. You're going to be busy.

MARY. Jim, what shall I order for you?

CONOVER. (*Looking at some telegrams.*) I'll have some chicken— and some coffee.

MARY. You can't have chicken and eat with us. I never want to see another chicken.

GRANT. Every time we sit down in a chair, somebody puts chicken in front of us. (*He pulls up trouser-leg and points to his calf.*) Look—pin-feathers!

CONOVER. All right, I'll have hamburger, too—hamburger and onions. (CONOVER *hands telegrams back to* SPIKE *and looks at paper over* GRANT'S *shoulder.*)

MARY. (*Into phone.*) Room service? (*Pause.*) This is room ——— (*She looks inquiringly toward men.*)

SPIKE. 2519. (SPIKE *crosses* R. *of desk.*)

MARY. 2519. Have you any hamburger? (*Pause.*) That's fine. Three hamburger steaks, one with onions—two without, dammit, and whatever goes with it—except spinach. (*To the men.*) Anybody want dessert? Ice cream's always safe.

GRANT. Fine!

CONOVER. None for me.

MARY. (*Into phone.*) One chocolate ice-cream. And three coffees. Will you hurry it, please? (*She hangs up. There is a knock on door.*) Come in! (BELLBOY *enters with* GRANT'S *bags. He is followed by* WAITER, *with tray of drinks. To* BELLBOY.) Put all the bags in there. (*She indicates* R. *bedroom. To* CONOVER—*taking cocktail from tray.*) We ordered a highball for you, Jim. (MARY *sits in chair in front of desk and drinks her cocktail.*)

CONOVER. Thanks. (WAITER *crosses to* SPIKE *with drink.*)

SPIKE. Are you the floor waiter?

WAITER. Yes, sir.

SPIKE. There's a dinner order in. Hurry it up for us, will you? (SPIKE *addresses* GRANT.) I've got a lot of people lined up for you to see, Grant.

GRANT. (*Crossing to* C. *and taking cocktail from* WAITER.) Can't I see them after the banquet? (WAITER *crosses to small table* R. *of sofa and starts fixing highball.*)

SPIKE. You were supposed to see them this afternoon, but you didn't get in, so I bunched them all between seven and seven-thirty.

CONOVER. Well, I can't have dinner here if a lot of people are coming in.

SPIKE. (*Crossing to* C.) No, it's O. K. I can keep this room clear. I'll juggle the visiting firemen between the two bedrooms. . . .

(*He points to two bedrooms.*) Grant can duck in and say hello, and come back and eat. We'll clear them all up in a hurry. (*He crosses back* R. CONOVER *crosses to couch and sits* R. end. BELLBOY *enters from* R. *bedroom.*)

BELLBOY. I've turned off the radiator and closed the windows. Anything else I can do?

GRANT. No, thanks. (GRANT *tips* BELLBOY, *who then exits.* WAITER *serves* CONOVER'S *highball, then crosses to* GRANT C., *who takes check and writes on it.*)

CONOVER. Grant, are you touching on labor again tonight?

GRANT. No!

MARY. (*Rising quickly and crossing to* GRANT.) Grant, we won't have time to dress after dinner. We ought to be changing now.

GRANT. (*Looking at watch.*) Yes, we can be changed by the time dinner gets here. (WAITER *starts out and* MARY *stops him.*)

MARY. Waiter! Another drink, Jim? (GRANT *crosses to desk and picks up coat.*)

CONOVER. No, thanks.

MARY. Spike?

SPIKE. Not now.

MARY. How about you, Grant? Another cocktail while you're dressing?

GRANT. I don't dare. I've got to make a speech. (*He finishes his cocktail and puts glass on desk.*)

MARY. (*To* WAITER *while placing her empty cocktail glass on tray.*) Well, bring another martini to the bedroom. (*She indicates room* R.)

WAITER. Right away, Ma'am. (WAITER *exits.*)

MARY. (*Crossing to* R. *bedroom.*) That's the difference between Grant and me—I'd rather be tight than be President. (MARY *exits into bedroom* R.)

GRANT. (*Crossing down* R. *to bedroom door.*) Spike, we haven't opened all those telegrams. Look through them, will you? (GRANT *starts to exit.* SPIKE *crosses to* L. *of desk.*)

CONOVER. Grant, while you're dressing, have you got a copy of your speech that I could be glancing at?

GRANT. (*At bedroom door.*) It's not a set speech, Jim. I'm just talking from notes.

CONOVER. (*Rising and crossing to* C.) Could I be looking over the notes?

43

GRANT. They're just some memos I scribbled down—I'm sorry, Jim, they wouldn't mean a thing to you. (SPIKE *has picked up telegrams.*) I'll tell you what you can read. Spike, show him some more of my fan mail. (GRANT *exits into* R. *bedroom,* SPIKE *throws wires on desk in disgust and turns to look at* CONOVER.)

CONOVER. You're a hell of a campaign manager!

SPIKE. That's why I wired for you. He's gotten away from me.

CONOVER. It's a damn shame! The boys in the Northwest and all along the Coast—they were swinging right in behind him. Then he had to stick out his chin in Wichita.

SPIKE. How much damage has he done?

CONOVER. We may have lost any chance for the labor vote. I must have had thirty calls after that speech. How did you let that happen?

SPIKE. (*Crossing to* CONOVER C.) I talked him out of that labor stuff in Denver—that is, I gave him something to use instead—local stuff—Rocky Mountain stuff.

CONOVER. Didn't you get a look at the speech for Wichita?

SPIKE. No, and I'll tell you why. She—(*He points to* R. *bedroom.*) —knew he was planning to talk about labor in Denver and when he didn't, she spent the rest of the night tossing harpoons into him. But the next day on the plane to Wichita they were clubby as hell—and I couldn't get any advance copy of the speech. You just sent the wrong dame with him!

CONOVER. (*Crossing to couch and sitting* R.) I even talked him into taking her along.

SPIKE. (*Crossing upstage* C.) When we get back to New York, Kay can straighten him out. But that doesn't help us tonight.

CONOVER. What are you afraid of tonight?

SPIKE. I don't know—(*Phone rings.*)—only she's too damn happy. (SPIKE *crosses to phone and speaks into it.*) Hello. (*Pause.*) Oh—give me the desk. (*To* CONOVER.) That's why I sent for you. We can't take a chance on his making another mistake. (*Into phone.*) Hello. This is MacManus. There are some people down there to see Mr. Matthews. And there are a lot more coming. Will you shoot 'em up to the 25th floor, Parlor B, and tell them to wait for me there? Thanks! (*He bangs up.* To CONOVER.) You've got to find out what he's talking about here. (SPIKE *picks up telegrams and crosses to couch, sitting* L.)

44

CONOVER. That's what I was trying to do—and you saw how far I got.

SPIKE. Well, keep after him.

CONOVER. If you've got people coming to see him, what chance have I?

SPIKE. (*Sitting L. end of couch.*) I wasn't sure you were going to get here. I figured I had to put some kind of pressure on him. I've got everybody—dairy farmers, automobile people, even the Labor boys, mad as they are.

CONOVER. Maybe they ought to be talking to Mrs. Matthews?

SPIKE. Look, Jim, this guy's vulnerable. He's got the bug.

CONOVER. That's what I was counting on. How bad has he got it?

SPIKE. He wants to be President, all right. So what I keep throwing at him is votes—get those votes—don't lose those votes. (CONOVER *rises and crosses to C., staring at bedroom R. SPIKE has by now read two or three wires.*) Say, maybe that Wichita speech didn't do as much harm as we thought it did?

CONOVER. Oh, those are just from people.

SPIKE. They don't count, eh?

CONOVER. (*Turning to SPIKE.*) You don't see any signed " State Chairman," do you?

SPIKE. Don't kid yourself, this guy does something to people. I've been on a lot of campaigns. They don't shake hands with Grant just to say they've shaken hands with him. They're up there with a light in their eyes—they practically mob him. If he gets away from us, you may be heading a " Stop Matthews " movement.

CONOVER. Stopping him wouldn't be any trouble. He hasn't any organization. I don't want to stop him. I think we can nominate him, if we can keep him in line. (SPIKE *has read another telegram.*)

SPIKE. Say, Jim, did you arrange this?

CONOVER. What?

SPIKE. He's speaking in New York—the twenty-third—Foreign Policy Association.

CONOVER. The hell he is! Why doesn't he consult us? (*Looks off R., at bedroom door.*)

SPIKE. (*Rising and crossing to* CONOVER.) He didn't even mention it to me. Just because I don't trust him doesn't mean he shouldn't trust me.

45

CONOVER. That forces us right out into the open. What's that date?

SPIKE. The twenty-third.

CONOVER. He can't speak there and pretend he's not a candidate. Besides that, he's got to go along with us on foreign policy. (*Hopefully.*) There's an issue around there somewhere, if we can just find it. We've got to make a strong play for the foreign vote. Well, I guess we've got to fence him in. Damn! (*He crosses L.*)

SPIKE. (*Following* CONOVER.) He wants that nomination. He wants to be President.

CONOVER. (*Turning to* SPIKE.) Then I'd better face him with some people who can deliver delegates—people he knows he has to have to win—I'd like to throw them at him all at once.

SPIKE. Better line up a big shot from labor.

CONOVER. Yes—Bill Hardy would do that for me. I could get Senator Lauterback to scare hell out of him on the farm vote.

SPIKE. You'd better have Kay there. I know damn well he listens to her.

CONOVER. Who would talk for business? Look around at the banquet tonight, Spike, and see if there's anybody who could be useful. (*A knock at door.*)

SPIKE. Damn it. I told them to send everybody to Parlor B. (*He goes to door and opens it. It is the* WAITER.)

WAITER. I have the dinner—and the extra cocktail.

SPIKE. Wheel it in! (WAITER *wheels in table with service for three and* MARY'S *second cocktail to* L. C. SPIKE *goes to bedroom door and knocks, after dropping telegrams on desk.*)

GRANT. (*Off.*) Yes?

SPIKE. Dinner's here.

GRANT. (*Off.*) We'll be right out.

SPIKE. Does Mary want her other cocktail in there?

MARY. (*Opening door.*) Cocktails don't have to come to me. I come to them. (MARY *enters in a dinner dress. She leaves door open.* WAITER *crosses to* MARY *and serves her cocktail.*)

WAITER. I have the dinner right outside. (*He exits and returns immediately with portable oven which he places against* L. *end of desk.*)

SPIKE. Grant, your room free?

GRANT. (*Off.*) All set. I'm just tying my tie.

46

SPIKE. When you're through will you unlock the hall door to your room?

GRANT. (Off.) Okay.

MARY. (To WAITER.) Serve it as soon as you're ready.

SPIKE. (Hurriedly crossing to L. bedroom.) I'd better unlock the hall door to this room, too. (SPIKE exits into L. bedroom. WAITER starts placing chairs at table L. C., chair from R. at R. of table. Chair from desk at C.—armchair from L. stage at L. MARY crosses to D. R. C.)

CONOVER. (Crossing to MARY.) My dear, that's a little unfair.

MARY. What?

CONOVER. I'm afraid that instead of listening to Grant they'll be just looking at you tonight.

MARY. Thank you, Jim. I'm so willing to believe that I'm going to pretend you're not a politician. (SPIKE returns from L. bedroom, closing door.)

SPIKE. (Crossing below table.) All right. Here we go. I'll bring in the first batch of patriots. (To MARY.) Remind Grant they've got votes. (Crosses up C.)

MARY. Spike does take the nobility out of a crusade.

SPIKE. (At doorway, with door open.) Am I supposed to be noble? On my salary! (He exits.)

CONOVER. Why don't you just spend the evening here with me? You've probably read Grant's speech anyway, haven't you?

MARY. I'm sorry you won't be there.

CONOVER. I'll listen to it on the radio—if I can get a radio—and if I can't—what's he speaking about?

MARY. Oh, I think we can get you a radio. (She goes to phone. GRANT enters from R. bedroom, closing door. CONOVER crosses to chair L. of dinner table.)

GRANT. I damn near left these notes in my other suit! (He starts looking through notes.)

MARY. (Into phone.) Could you have a radio sent up to 2519 right away? (Pause.) It's very important. (Pause.) Thank you! (She hangs up.) It looks as though you'll have to listen, Jim. They think you can have one.

CONOVER. (To GRANT.) If you want to rehearse any of that, Grant, I'll be glad to have you try it out on me.

GRANT. I'll give you the start —— (Speaks as though he were addressing a large audience.) Ladies—(Looks toward MARY then

47

turns to CONOVER.)—and members of the Automotive Council of Detroit. I know that I am among friends here tonight—and it would be unfriendly of me not to talk to you with utter frankness and naked honesty. In the economic anarchy we are facing to-day ——

WAITER. (*Rising, with plate from portable oven.*) Who's with onions?

CONOVER. I'm with onions. (MARY *goes to* C. *place at table. The two men go to either side.* GRANT *at* R. *and* CONOVER *on* L. WAITER *puts the " with onions " in* CONOVER'S *place and the other plate in hand in front of* MARY.)

WAITER. Watch the plates—they are very hot.

GRANT. Looks good—I can hardly wait. Waiter, you've got a starving man on your hands. (WAITER *serves* GRANT.)

WAITER. I will bring the dessert in fifteen minutes. Watch the plate. (WAITER *exits with oven.*)

GRANT. Ah—meat! And can I use it! (*He has his knife and fork poised when* R. *bedroom door opens and* SPIKE *enters.*)

SPIKE. Grant, your public is waiting.

GRANT. My hamburger's waiting.

SPIKE. Hamburgers don't vote. These are dairy farmers. (*He crosses to* GRANT *and hands him a list, pointing to name at top.*) The fellow with the moustache is the one to play for.

GRANT. Just the Number Five handshake, Spike?

SPIKE. No, a little talk. You know—cows, butter, milk, cheese— since the war American cheese has become big industry ——

GRANT. What do I know about American cheese?

SPIKE. Walk this way and meet three perfect specimens. (GRANT *rises and starts to door.*) Remember —— (GRANT *turns.*) They got votes! (GRANT *exits into bedroom* R., *indicating door* L.) Well—now I'll set 'em up in the other alley. (*He exits* U. C.)

MARY. (*Turning to* CONOVER.) Jim, how do you think Grant's doing? What are your reports?

CONOVER. First let me tell you about my reports on you. You've done a great job, and I want to congratulate you.

MARY. Well, I'd like to admit something, if I could be sure it wouldn't be used against me. I've enjoyed it—every minute of it.

CONOVER. Even the speeches?

MARY. That's been the best part of it. I don't mean just listening to Grant. I mean listening to the people—feeling the way they respond. Of course they laugh and yell when he talks about the troubles he had during the war getting things through in Washington . . .

CONOVER. (*Busily eating.*) Yes, I've heard those laughs. He does it very cleverly. That's what they like to hear.

MARY. Jim, over the radio you only hear the audience when it's making noise. What you don't hear is the silence—when Grant has them so they're not thinking of themselves—when he has them thinking of the country—that's when it takes your breath away.

CONOVER. I'm glad Grant can do that. I know how effective it can be in a speaker.

MARY. (*Brushing him aside.*) Jim, I'm not talking about Grant. When they rush up after the speeches—I wish you could see their faces. . . . You know, I'd forgotten how good it is to be with people—I used to see a lot of them when Grant first started and had small plants—when we moved to New York I got too far away from them—they're so eager to do whatever is the best thing to do—and they're so quick—they're so intelligent. (*She laughs.*) They've thrown a couple of questions at Grant that had him stopped cold. He just had to admit he didn't know enough to answer them. And they liked him for it.

CONOVER. That's smart. Shows he uses his head.

MARY. (*Sitting back in chair and regarding* CONOVER *quizzically.*) Jim, you fascinate me. You have such a complete lack of faith in sincerity—and you're so sincere about it. (CONOVER *gives her an understanding smile.*) What puzzles me is that I dislike so thoroughly the way your mind works—and yet I'm so very fond of you.

CONOVER. It is puzzling, isn't it, because I feel the same way toward you. (*She pats his hand with fond reproof.*)

MARY. You're so cynical. (CONOVER *pats her hand in same manner.*)

CONOVER. You're so unrealistic. (*They grin at each other.* GRANT *enters from* R. *bedroom.*)

MARY. (*To* GRANT.) Well, how's the farmer's choice?

GRANT. (*Crossing and standing at table.*) After the beautiful things I have just said about cows, I shouldn't touch this hamburger. It's like eating an old friend. But I'm going to. (*He sits down and gets ready to cut hamburger.* SPIKE *enters from* L. *bedroom.*)

49

SPIKE. Ah, back from the pastures! Wipe off your feet and come in and meet the A. F. of L.

GRANT. Look, Spike, give me a chance to eat ——

SPIKE. Nope. This is a crisis. I have to know you're holding the A. F. of L. in there while I sneak the C. I. O. into the other bedroom. (*He points to* R. *bedroom.*)

GRANT. Put them both in the same room. I'll talk to them both at the same time.

SPIKE. Little Boy Blue, haven't you heard? They ain't keeping steady company any more. Besides these aren't big shots—just small fry—officers in the local.

GRANT. They're both Labor groups. They both want the same things. That's what I've been talking about all this time—getting people to work together—now let's put it into action.

SPIKE. Now, boss ——

GRANT. Spike, I'm serious about this. Tell those men in there you're bringing in the C. I. O. and then I'll come in and talk to them! (SPIKE *shrugs and exits into* L. *bedroom.* MARY *preens herself, looking proudly from* GRANT *to* CONOVER.)

CONOVER. Grant, aren't you just asking for trouble?

GRANT. Jim, I've got both organizations working in my plants. I can walk into a recreation room where C. I. O. and A. F. of L. men are there together and talk to them—talk Labor to them. Bill Green and Phil Murray will both sit down with each other. Most of the big boys in Labor are all right, except for Lewis. (*He points to* L. *bedroom.*) This is the type of men we've got to get together.

CONOVER. I don't mind you having your head in the clouds—but I wish you'd keep your feet in the voting booth.

GRANT. Jim, these men in the next room are the kind who are responsible for wildcat strikes. If I can make them see something bigger than their jobs as heads of their own locals, and the little power they get from that . . .

MARY. (*To* CONOVER.) There may be some votes in that, too.

CONOVER. One of the things I came down to talk to you about— I got a very bad reaction to your speech in Wichita.

GRANT. Did you read any of those telegrams?

CONOVER. You may have picked up a few votes there in the auditorium—but you've chilled off most of the Labor leaders in the country—I know! I've talked to them!

50

GRANT. I said that Labor had to have a fairer share of the profits. That didn't chill them off, did it?

CONOVER. No—that was all right—for Labor.

GRANT. I said that both management and Labor had to stop treating each other as enemies and start treating each other as partners. Did they object to that?

CONOVER. No, damn it—it was your stirring up union members against their leaders.

GRANT. Jim, what I said was—one of the biggest causes of labor trouble is that *wherever the members don't run the union, the union runs the members.*

CONOVER. That's it—you don't think the labor leaders enjoyed hearing that, do you?

GRANT. I told them, Jim—I had to tell them—that if the individual union member had accepted his responsibility in his union and had made it a democratic union, and not just handed over his power to the leaders, there wouldn't have been any reason for the Taft-Hartley Act.

CONOVER. There had to be some labor legislation.

GRANT. Of course there had to be. But it's their own fault that it was that drastic. If they want the Taft-Hartley Act repealed let them clean up the conditions that gave Congress the excuse to pass it.

CONOVER. Grant, that's no way to talk to them, we need those votes.

GRANT. Jim, I'm not so interested in the men they vote for for President or Congress as I am in the men they vote for for officers in their own unions.

CONOVER. You get too damn specific. For instance, did you have to say it was a good thing for unions to have to open their books?

GRANT. Some of the biggest and best unions in the country had already opened their books.

MARY. Jim, in Wichita the audience was full of union men—I don't mean union leaders, I mean union members, and they cheered Grant. I have a feeling they'll be glad to get a look at those books themselves.

CONOVER. (*Sulkily.*) Well, some of that money went into campaign contributions. (SPIKE *enters from* L. *bedroom. They look at him.*)

GRANT. Well?

SPIKE. (*At door* L.) No dice. They're even mad they're in the same hotel together.

GRANT. That makes me pretty mad, too.

SPIKE. Boss, you've got to speak to them.

GRANT. (*Throws down napkin, rises and crosses to* L. *bedroom door.*) Of course I'll speak to them. How am I going to do what I want to do if I don't speak to them?

SPIKE. Here are the names. (*He hands* GRANT *a list.*) Watch out for the little guy they call Mac. (GRANT *angrily grabs paper and exits into* L. *bedroom.*) Now for some counter-espionage. (SPIKE *crosses above table to hall door and exits.*)

MARY. Jim, Grant's got something. Don't take it away from him. When he's just cockeyed drunk with sincerity people can't resist him.

CONOVER. That statement sounds as though it includes you, too.

MARY. Well, let me straighten you out about Grant and me. Our personal relations are strictly political. (*She starts eating again.*)

CONOVER. I thought I saw Grant throw a look or two at you tonight that wasn't entirely impersonal.

MARY. (*Looking at* CONOVER.) Jim, you're a bachelor, aren't you?

CONOVER. Theoretically. Why?

MARY. It's just that if you'd been married, you'd understand.

CONOVER. Understand what?

MARY. When a man and woman have been married for a long time even their closest friends can't always tell whether they're still in love with each other. They themselves wonder about it sometimes.

CONOVER. Well, then the trip's accomplished something—if you're at the point of wondering.

MARY. No, there are things that happen that make you sure— little things that don't really mean anything except that you know how much they do mean. For instance, Grant found out once the girls at school used to call me Maizie. He knew I hated it. So sometimes he used to call me Maizie—just to tease me—but you don't tease people that way unless you love each other. Well, Maizie doesn't live here any more. And another thing—Grant always hated to hear me swear—whenever I let go with something —he used to smack me on the behind—hard. I've done a lot of swearing on this trip ——

CONOVER. (*With mock sympathy.*) And no smacks?

52

MARY. (*Wistfully*.) It's a small request—but I'd give anything for a good smack on the behind.

CONOVER. I certainly wish there were something I could do about that. (SPIKE *enters from* R. *bedroom*.)

SPIKE. Still in with them? (*He points to* L. *bedroom*.)

MARY. Yes, and all's quiet on the Western front.

SPIKE. Well, the Eastern front is ready. (GRANT *enters from* L. *bedroom, closing door behind him*.)

GRANT. (*To* SPIKE.) Are the C. I. O. boys in there?

SPIKE. Yes—and in what I would call an ugly mood.

GRANT. Keep your back turned, Jim. (CONOVER *turns head* U. S. *and* GRANT *opens* L. *bedroom door*.) This way, gentlemen. (*He starts across the stage. Opens* R. *bedroom door and steps back into room. Enter from* L. *bedroom three stony-faced* LABOR LEADERS. MARY *springs up and crosses down to* R. *to greet them*.) This is Mrs. Matthews! (MARY *extends hand*.) Mr. Vincent.

MARY. (*Shaking hands*.) How do you do? (VINCENT *shakes hands and keeps going toward* R. *bedroom door*.)

GRANT. Mr. Solly. (SOLLY *and* MARY *shake hands*.)

MARY. How do you do?

GRANT. Mr. Mack. (MACK *and* MARY *shake hands*.)

MARY. How do you do?

GRANT. Right in here, gentlemen. (*They file in*. GRANT *turns and gives a broad wink to* MARY *and* CONOVER, *and follows in after them, closing door*. SPIKE *puts his fingers in his ears and stands shuddering as though he expects an explosion, then relaxes with a grin*.)

SPIKE. You know, Grant might be able to unite the United Nations. (SPIKE *exits* U. C.)

MARY. Poor Grant. He's not getting a thing to eat. (*She crosses to desk and gets a cigarette from her evening bag*.)

CONOVER. I was hoping we three could have a quiet dinner together and talk.

MARY. We'll see you after we get back here.

CONOVER. I'd like to go over with Grant what he's speaking about tonight. Tell me something about it.

MARY. Well, it's his last speech of the trip. (*She lights her cigarette*.) It's sort of a summary.

CONOVER. Detroit's a dangerous city politically—almost anything you say here is controversial.

MARY. (*Crossing to above chair* C. *at table.*) Isn't a Presidential campaign supposed to be controversial?

CONOVER. Yes, but they've had a lot of trouble here—strikes—race riots—and for some reason or other it seems to be the headquarters of the lunatic fringe.

MARY. You mean the subversive groups ——

CONOVER. Mary, subversive is a very dangerous word—(*Apprehensively.*)—Grant's not using that word in his speech tonight, is he?

MARY. I think Grant's saving anything like that—and the international situation—for his speech in New York.

CONOVER. Oh, is he speaking in New York?

MARY. Yes! (GRANT *enters from* R. *bedroom.*) Still alive?

GRANT. Yes, and so are they. (*Crosses to table.*) As a matter of fact, the Congress of Industrial Organizations has just extended an invitation to the American Federation of Labor to have a glass of beer.

CONOVER. (*With a bit of a grin.*) Under whose jurisdiction?

GRANT. (*Sitting at his place at table.*) The Arcade Bar and Grill! (*He starts to eat.*)

CONOVER. Mary tells me you're making a speech in New York?

GRANT. (*Gratified.*) Yes. The twenty-third. Foreign Policy Association! That's moving into the big time!

CONOVER. You couldn't postpone that, could you? I don't see how you can open up on the International situation and still pretend you're not a candidate.

GRANT. I didn't think I could turn it down.

CONOVER. Well, it's too late, I guess. (*Disturbed.*) I couldn't very well advise you about something I didn't know anything about. (SPIKE *enters from* L. *bedroom.*)

SPIKE. O. K., Grant, if you're ready!

GRANT. (*Starting to eat again.*) Spike, they can't be more important than this hamburger.

SPIKE. Well, they're all your friends. It's the Detroit tycoon set.

GRANT. (*Rising with alacrity.*) Oh, somebody I really want to see? You're slipping, Spike. (*He crosses and exits into* L. *bedroom.*)

SPIKE. I've got one more set. These are gate crashers. Even I don't know who they are.

MARY. (*Dousing cigarette.*) I wonder whether I have time to sneak a look in a mirror?

54

SPIKE. Sure you have. (*She starts for* R. *bedroom.* SPIKE *exiting to door sees* GRANT'S *food, sits in* GRANT'S *place and picks up knife and fork, prepared to eat.*)

MARY. (*Turns to speak to* CONOVER.) Oh, Jim —— (*She sees* SPIKE.) Spike, don't you dare touch that! (SPIKE *rises.*)

SPIKE. All right, I can starve. (*Shakes his finger at* MARY.) But that's the way you make Communists. (*He exits through door to hall.*)

MARY. Jim, before Grant gets back I wanted to thank you for telling him the gossip about me.

CONOVER. I didn't tell him.

MARY. Well, somebody must have told him.

CONOVER. Has he said anything?

MARY. No, but he's very rude to all army majors. (CONOVER *chuckles.*) And it's so unfair to those poor majors. My Major's been a Colonel for months.

CONOVER. (*Rising.*) I hadn't heard about that.

MARY. Jim, your secret service works backwards. They keep secrets from you! (GRANT *enters from* L. *bedroom.*)

GRANT. Mary, Sam Parrish is in here. He'd like to say hello to you.

MARY. Good! I haven't seen Sam for ages. (*She starts* L.)

CONOVER.. Wait, Mary! Grant, I'd like to have a few words with Parrish myself. Could you have him step in here?

GRANT. Sure, I'll tell him.

CONOVER. Oh, Grant—don't let the others know I'm here. (GRANT *exits into* L. *bedroom.* CONOVER *moves up* L. *out of range of door, pulling his chair with him.*)

MARY. We've known Sam for years. We're very fond of him.

CONOVER. So am I. He's raised a lot of money for the Party. (SAM PARRISH *enters from* L. *bedroom, closing door after him. He sees* MARY *and crosses to her.*)

SAM. Hello, Mary! You're a sight for sore eyes! (*He kisses* MARY.)

MARY. Hello, Sam!

SAM. Mary, I'll be in New York for our annual dinner on the 17th. This time it's on me!

MARY. No, Sam, you're having dinner with us.

SAM. My, you're just as pretty as you ever were! I could eat you with a spoon. . . . (*He catches sight of* CONOVER.) Why, Jim Conover, you old son-of-a-gun! (*He crosses to* CONOVER.)

55

CONOVER. Hi-ya, Sam!

SAM. What are you doing here?

CONOVER. Take it easy, Sam. You're the only one in Detroit who knows I AM here—and keep it to yourself!

SAM. What the hell's going on? Say —— (*He looks from* CONOVER *to* MARY *and then toward* L. *bedroom.*) Damn it, I might have known. I'm due in Washington on the 18th. I had it all planned to come and see you to sell you the idea that we need a business man in the White House and that man is Grant Matthews, and, damn it, you beat me to it. Frankly I was going to bribe you with the biggest campaign contribution you ever saw.

CONOVER. (*Grabbing* SAM'S *hand and shaking it.*) That's a date, Sam! Lunch in Washington on the 18th, and bring cash!

SAM. (*Gleefully, crossing to* MARY.) Mary, you go right home and start packing. You're moving into the White House. Give me another kiss! (*He kisses* MARY *again.*) I've never been so happy about anything in my life. Wait until I tell Hilda!

CONOVER. Sam, you're not telling anybody, including Hilda.

MARY. How is Hilda? Is she coming to the banquet?

SAM. No, damn it, she's in bed with the flu. She's so mad she's going to miss Grant's speech she's not fit to live with. Look—why don't you call her up? Niagara 2956.

MARY. I'd better call her now because I'm not sure you and Hilda will be speaking to us after Grant's speech tonight. (MARY *goes to phone and picks up receiver.*)

CONOVER. (*Stepping* U. R.—*to* MARY, *sharply.*) Why do you say that?

SAM. (*Crossing to* CONOVER.) The last time I was in New York, Grant and I had a hell of a knockdown dragout fight about profits and high prices.

CONOVER. (*To* MARY.) Mary, is that what Grant's talking about tonight? (*He crosses to above table,* SAM *follows him.*)

MARY. (*Into phone.*) Just a minute. (*To* SAM.) What's that number again, Sam?

SAM. Niagara 2956.

MARY. (*Into phone.*) Niagara 2956.

SAM. (L. *of* CONOVER.) You know Grant—likes to talk like a radical. But hell, anybody that's made as much money as Grant has is a sound American. (GRANT *enters from* L. *bedroom.*)

GRANT. (*Crossing to* SAM *and putting arm around his shoulder.*)

56

The other boys thought they ought to hurry over there, Sam. Why don't you stick around a while and go over with us?

SAM. No, I've got to go with them. I'm chairman of the Committee. (*He starts for bedroom door* L. *but* GRANT *stops him.*)

GRANT. (*Crossing below and leading* SAM *to door* U. C.) You can catch them at the elevator. I'll let you out this way.

SAM. (*Following* GRANT, *who opens hall door.*) I'll come back after the banquet. Got something to talk to you about, eh, Jim. (*He gives* CONOVER *a wink, then to* GRANT.) That was a hell of a good speech you made in Wichita. I could go along with two-thirds of it—especially that stuff about strikes. The other third— I suppose you've got to say those things—but look out people don't get the idea you're too far to the left. Tell you what—you take a crack at Walter Reuther tonight and you'll make a hell of a hit. But I don't need to tell you that. Talk to you about it later.

MARY. (*Into phone.*) Keep trying and call me when you get them. (*She bangs up.*)

SAM. See you later, Mary.

MARY. Good-bye, Sam.

SAM. (*Shaking hands with* GRANT.) Damn it, Grant! I'll be telling people I knew you when.

GRANT. Don't tell them yet!

SAM. (*Outside door.*) Hey, wait! Going down! (SAM *exits and* GRANT *closes door after him.*)

CONOVER. (*Accusingly, standing* L. *of table.*) You're talking about profits and high prices tonight?

GRANT. (*Crossing down* C.) Touching on them, among other things. (*He lights cigarette.*)

CONOVER. What angle are you taking?

GRANT. We talked about it in Washington. You know how I stand.

CONOVER. In Washington you were pretty specific. You're not being that specific here tonight?

GRANT. You're damn right I am!

CONOVER. What are you going to say?

GRANT. I'm going to tell them this . . . they talk about how they want to save the private enterprise system, now they've got a chance to do it.

CONOVER. Yes . . . ?

GRANT. Well, they're not going to save it if they restrict production just to keep prices high. If they're going to sacrifice the consumer just to pile up profits they're going to wreck the private enterprise system, not save it.

CONOVER. Grant, you can't say things like that to this crowd. You're talking to wealthy men. Why antagonize them?

GRANT. Jim, you know reconversion should have gone deeper than just retooling our plants. We need a moral reconversion. Take what big business is hoping to do with the tariff—what they tried to do on wool. They'd like to see prosperity become an American monopoly. Jim, there won't be any United Nations if America is the only prosperous country in a starving world.

CONOVER. Damn it, Grant, if you're going to be a candidate you can't come out against prosperity.

GRANT. We can't have international peace if we declare economic war. You know that's what I think.

CONOVER. Grant, you can't say those things now, and you can't say them here. This town is one of my best sources for silent money.

GRANT. You'll have to take your chances on the silent money, Jim.*

MARY. (At desk.) What is silent money?

CONOVER. (Addressing GRANT.) I warn you, Grant, you can't get out on this limb before the nomination.

MARY. (Crossing to L. of GRANT.) The people ought to know where he stands before they nominate him.

CONOVER. (Angrily.) The people have damn little to say about the nomination. You two have lived in this country all your lives. Haven't you got that through your heads yet? You're not nominated by the people—you're nominated by the politicians! Why? Because the voters are too damned lazy to vote in the primaries! Well, politicians are not lazy.

GRANT. (Crossing to R. of table.) They've got to know what I think, Jim! I told you that from the start. I've got to be on record.

CONOVER. All right—but not here—not tonight! Later. When you're out in Nebraska or Oklahoma. (SPIKE enters from R. bedroom.)

SPIKE. Okay, Grant. This is the last group. And are they fruity!

CONOVER. Stall them, Spike. We're discussing something.

* Grant picks up cue immediately so that there is no interruption to the fight. Also rides over any laughs Conover might get in above scene.

GRANT. No, Jim. I'm seeing them. (CONOVER *sits in chair* c. *at table.* GRANT *turns to* SPIKE.) Who are they?

SPIKE. I don't know. They call themselves the Americans Incorruptible.

GRANT. (*Crossing* R.) I've never heard of them.

SPIKE. They're dressed for the McKinley campaign. I didn't take their names. The Head Incorruptible is the fat dame with the big cow-catcher.

GRANT. What's their angle? What are they for?

MARY. (*Crossing down to* L. *of* GRANT.) With a name like that they're not for anything. They're against something.

SPIKE. Yes. (*He takes* GRANT'S *cigarette away from him.*) Let's take no chances! But remember—they've got votes! (GRANT *opens door to* R. *bedroom, looks in, then turns back to* SPIKE.)

GRANT. They shouldn't have! (*He exits into* R. *bedroom.* MARY *crosses front to couch and picks up newspaper, starts reading editorial on* GRANT.)

SPIKE. I think I'd better go and air out Parlor B. (*He starts out. Phone rings.*)

MARY. That's probably Hilda Parrish for me.

SPIKE. (*Into phone.*) Hello. . . . This is MacManus. (*He shakes head negatively at* MARY. *To* CONOVER.) It's for you, Jim. (SPIKE *puts phone on desk and exits.* CONOVER *crosses to desk and picks up phone.*)

CONOVER. (*Into phone, casually, as though talking to an old political friend.*) Hello. Oh, hello, how are you? (*Pause.*) Who told you I was here—Sam? (*Pause.*) Where are you? (*Pause.*) All right. I'll come up to your room. (*He hangs up and turns to* MARY.) Mary, will you tell Grant ——? (*Phone rings again.*)

MARY. (*Drops paper and crosses to phone.*) That must be Hilda.

CONOVER. Tell Grant I'll be right back. (*He exits.*)

MARY. Right! (*Into phone.*) Hello. . . . Oh, hello, Hilda. (*Pause.*) This is Mary . . . Mary Matthews! (*Pause.*) Yes. I'm here with Grant. (WAITER *enters with one ice-cream and three coffees, starts to pour coffee.*) I'm so sorry you're sick. (*Pause.*) Well, if it isn't too much for you, we'd love to run out for a few minutes after the banquet. (*Pause.*) Good. Oh, Grant's in the next room with some women. (*Pause and laughs.*) No, he's safe. There's a whole committee of them. (*Pause.*) All right . . . see you later. Good-bye, dear. (MARY *hangs up and crosses to* WAITER R. *of table, who has check on tray.*) Have you the check?

WAITER. Yes, ma'am. (WAITER *hands* MARY *pencil and offers check on tray. She starts writing on check.*)

MARY. I'll write your tip on it.

WAITER. Is your husband Grant Matthews?

MARY. Yes.

WAITER. He certainly don't pull any punches, does he?

MARY. (*Smiling.*) You said that just in time. (*She writes tip on check,* WAITER *looks at it and smiles broadly.*)

WAITER. (*Big.*) Oh, thank you! (WAITER *hurries out.*)

GRANT. (*Entering from* R. *bedroom, carrying hat and coat. He places them on table* U. C.) Well, we've lost the Americans Incorruptible.

MARY. (*Taking cup of coffee.*) Who were they? What did they want?

GRANT. (*With sarcasm. Crossing down to chair* R. *of table.*) They think America's being too harsh on poor little Germany and Japan. We shouldn't have gotten into it in the first place!

MARY. Oh, that crowd! Against war—but we may have to fight the Russians!

GRANT. (*Sitting at table and starting on ice-cream.*) Exactly! I wound up making a campaign speech for Stalin. (*He looks around.*) Where's Jim?

MARY. (*Crossing down* L. *of table.*) He'll be back in a minute. He had a telephone call. Grant, what is silent money?

GRANT. Oh, it's a way they get around the Hatch Act.

MARY. What's the Hatch Act?

GRANT. It's a law they passed a few years ago about campaign contributions. Only individuals can give the money, and nobody more than $5,000, and you have to account for how it's spent. It's a very pretty law—and we feel very moral that it's on the books—but it just doesn't work.

MARY. There must have been some reason for passing it?

GRANT. Yes, there was! It had gotten to be a bad situation. But you know how we do things in this country, sometimes. When human nature gets to behaving like human nature, they pass a law repealing human nature. But the Hatch Act is too tough. So men who can afford it walk in and put silent money down on the barrelhead—cash, that can't be traced. It's been done by both parties before the law was passed and since. I've told you before, Mary, there's damn little difference between Democrats and Republicans.

MARY. Well, if silent money's illegal, I don't think you should take it!

GRANT. Oh, I wouldn't take it. That would be Jim's business.

MARY. But, Grant —— (*She puts her coffee cup on table.*)

GRANT. (*Stopping her.*) Now, Mary, we both drank during Prohibition, didn't we? Put it down to political education, the way the PAC does. (*Seeing she is still troubled.*) I can't be too righteous about taking silent money. I've given it.

MARY. If you take money, you have to pay it back some way.

GRANT. (*Indignant.*) Mary! You know damn well I'm not for sale!

MARY. You've arranged that very neatly in your mind, Grant. All they have to do is buy Conover. I warned you the Presidency was a great temptation.

GRANT. (*After a tight-lipped pause. He pushes food away and turns to face front.*) You certainly have a gift for making it tough for me. You didn't used to be that way.

MARY. (*Distressed with herself, crossing U. C. to D. R.*) I know. I hear myself saying those things. I suppose it's a gift I picked up in exchange for some illusions.

GRANT. (*With sober reasoning—turning to* MARY.) Mary, people change. We've both changed. Life does that to you. We would have been happier if we could have stayed the two kids who went on a honeymoon to Victoria. I'm just as unhappy as you are that we didn't. (*There is a pause.* MARY *takes a turn* U. R.)

MARY. I'm sorry Jim got a line on what you're going to say here.

GRANT. Yes, damn it! I was all keyed up for tonight's speech.

MARY. Are you going to change it?

GRANT. Oh, no! Don't worry. I'm going to speak my mind.

MARY. Grant, you have to! You told big labor they had to take the responsibility that goes with their power. You certainly have to be just as frank with big business.

GRANT. I'm going to! Jim's argument was just not to say it here in Detroit!

MARY. In Wichita you said what you really believed. (*She crosses to* GRANT'S *chair.*) Remember the satisfaction it gave you? I hope you feel that way tonight?

61

GRANT. I'd like to feel that way all the time. But you know yourself, you get into spots where you just can't afford it.

MARY. Grant—you know you don't have to be President.

GRANT. Oh—I don't even expect to be! (*Pause.*) But I know this much—I could do a lot of good.

MARY. (*Smoothing his hair.*) Well, you may have to make up your mind whether you want that inner satisfaction or —— (CONOVER *enters from outer hall.* MARY *crosses* R.)

GRANT. (*Rising and crossing to get coat from table* U. R. C.) Jim, where's Spike? It's getting late. We ought to be going.

CONOVER. He may be getting the car around. Grant, before you go I'd like to pick up where we left off about your speech tonight.

GRANT. (*Putting on coat.*) Jim, let's talk about my speech after I've made it. (SPIKE *enters from* L. *bedroom, crosses to* R. *of* GRANT.)

SPIKE. I hate to pull this on you, Grant, but there's one more delegation.

GRANT. To hell with them! Tell them I've left.

SPIKE. (*Handing slip of paper to* GRANT.) You can't do that. They might see you on your way out.

GRANT. (*Taking slip.*) Okay. (*He starts for* L. *bedroom.*)

MARY. Grant, we're the guests of honor. We can't be late.

GRANT. I'll make this short. Get your things, Mary. (GRANT *exits into* L. *bedroom.*)

SPIKE. Mary, you've got at least five minutes. I'll go down and check up on the police escort.

MARY. It's a wonderful country! You take the police along with you so they can help you break the speed laws. (*She exits into* R. *bedroom, leaving door open.* SPIKE *exits* U. C. CONOVER *wanders down to open door, speaking through it.*)

CONOVER. Take your time, Mary. The way you look tonight I want everybody there before you make your entrance.

MARY. (*Off.*) Don't be so flattering, Jim, or I'll think you want something from me!

CONOVER. (*Laughing.*) As a matter of fact, I do. I was just going to ask you a favor.

MARY. (*Entering from* R. *bedroom, wearing jacket to dress.*) Fine! What can I do for you?

CONOVER. You're having Sam Parrish to dinner on the 17th. Do **you** mind inviting me, too?

MARY. Why, no. I'd love to have you. (MARY *crosses to desk and picks up bag, then to chair* C. *of table.*)

CONOVER. Can I impose on you by inviting some other guests— say four or five?

MARY. (*Hesitating.*) I hadn't planned that kind of a party on the 17th ——

CONOVER. If Grant's speaking on the twenty-third on International Policy, it may be important for him to see these people first. (MARY *hesitates again, then comes to a decision.*)

MARY. All right, Jim. Do I know any of these people?

CONOVER. Well, you know Sam —— (*He crosses to* R. *of table.*) And there's one other I'd like to talk to you about. You remember the reason I wanted you to make this trip in the first place?

MARY. Yes, I remember well enough.

CONOVER. Mary, I've been looking into how that talk got started. Mrs. Thorndyke used to be a frequent guest at your house. Then about a year ago she was crossed off your list, but Grant went on seeing her?

MARY. Yes.

CONOVER. Let's kill off those rumors once and for all. I want Mrs. Thorndyke there on the 17th.

MARY. (*Outraged.*) No, Jim! Not in my house. And of all nights, not on the 17th! It happens to be our wedding anniversary.

CONOVER. Look, Mary, I'm doing my damnedest to go along with Grant, even though he doesn't always go along with me. I need Mrs. Thorndyke there for more reasons than one. Let me win this, will you?

MARY. I'm sorry, Jim; that's more than I can take. (*There is a knock on the door.*) Come in! (BELLBOY *enters with radio.*)

BELLBOY. Here's your radio. I had to steal it from another room.

MARY. That's fine. Can you connect it for us?

CONOVER. (*Crossing* D. R.) Let's talk about this some more after the banquet. (BELLBOY *puts radio on desk, unwinding cord.* GRANT *enters from* L. *bedroom.*)

MARY. (*To* GRANT.) Ready! (GRANT *takes a swig of coffee.*)

BELLBOY. Everybody wanted a radio tonight.

GRANT. (*Pleased.*) So?

BELLBOY. Special broadcast from Hollywood—Bob Hope and Jack Benny. (*He plugs cord in behind* U. R. *end of desk.*)

GRANT. Yes, I've got a break tonight, Jim—I'm following Hope and Benny. (MARY *crosses to table* U. R. C. *to get his hat.*)

MARY. (*Handing* GRANT *his hat.*) After all that nonsense they'll be glad to hear Grant make sense. (*Door opens and* SPIKE *sticks his head in.* BELLBOY *turns on radio.*)

SPIKE. All set? I've got the elevator waiting for you.

MARY. (*Excitedly.*) Grant, fix your tie. Listen in, Jim. You'll find out what Grant's talking about!

GRANT. Good-bye, Jim. (GRANT *and* MARY *exit hurriedly.*)

CONOVER. Good luck. (MARY *rushes back in a minute in great excitement, holding her bag in her* R. *hand.*)

MARY. Where's my bag, my bag, my bag?

CONOVER. What's that in your hand?

MARY. (*Staring at bag.*) That's my bag! (*She wheels around and runs out.* BELLBOY *turns off radio and crosses* D. S. *to* CONOVER.)

BELLBOY. (*Referring to radio.*) Works all right. Do you want it on?

CONOVER. No. I can turn a radio on—and off. (*He tips* BELLBOY, *who thanks him and exits.* CONOVER *pulls chair from table* R. *and places it* R. *of desk, then crosses to bedroom* L. *and opens door.*) We may as well sit in here and be comfortable! (KAY THORNDYKE *enters and goes to chair* R. *of desk. She sits down.* CONOVER *brings over other chair and places it* L. *of desk.*) I have a radio. Do I dare listen?

KAY. I think so. Of course I had less than five minutes with him.

CONOVER. Yes. And Mary's had five weeks! (*He starts to light a cigar.*)

KAY. I think he was glad to see me. I told you in Washington I could handle him.

CONOVER. Well, we'll find out. (*He sits down chair* L. *of desk.*)

KAY. I made it pretty strong. I said the Democrats would never take a chance like that. But that brought up a question that's on his mind, Jim, and you'd better have an answer ready for him.

CONOVER. An answer to what?

KAY. Is there any real difference between the Democratic Party and the Republican Party?

CONOVER. That's a hell of a question for a Presidential candidate to ask! All the difference in the world. They're in—and we're out! (*He turns on radio.*)

CURTAIN

64

ACT III

SCENE 1

The living-room of the Matthews' apartment in New York. It is a large room, the entrance from the hall being from an arch upstage, somewhat L. of C.; the door from the elevator being somewhere offstage L. The hall continues to R. to other rooms in the apartment and we can see stairs which suggest it is a duplex. Above R. arch there is a bar, and to R. of that presumably an entrance to the dining-room. The door to a powder-room or guest bedroom is down L. off the living-room. There is a fireplace in R. wall. R. C. half of stage is occupied by a sofa, and a large ottoman below fireplace. Extreme L. are two chairs turned toward each other with a small table between them. There is a painting of MARY *and the* CHILDREN C. *wall, and below it is a chest of drawers, with tables and lamps at either end, and 2 straight chairs R. and L. of those.*

DISCOVERED: *At rise:* SPIKE *is sitting on L. end of the sofa. There is a liquor bottle package at his feet. He has also an ashtray at his feet and is busy crossing off names on a list.* SWENSON, *the butler, is standing L., facing* SPIKE, *with a piece of note-paper in his hand and a pencil.* SPIKE *has the one list in his hand and a diagram is on the couch beside him. Each contains a list of the invited guests.*

SPIKE. Judge Alexander—bourbon—bourbon and plain water— he may take a cocktail, but I doubt it—he'll probably stick to straight bourbon.
SWENSON. Yes, sir. (*He makes a note.*)
SPIKE. Now his wife—do you know how to mix a Sazarac?
SWENSON. No, sir, but I can look it up.
SPIKE. Well, I'll tell you. Take an old-fashioned glass and put a lump of sugar in it, soaked in Pernod.
SWENSON. I don't think we have any Pernod, sir.

SPIKE. I brought some. It's in there. (*He points to package.*)
Then a jigger of bourbon, a twist of lemon-peel on the top and
give it a good stir. Don't sample that one, Swenson, it'll light up
your vest buttons. (SWENSON *has made a note,* SPIKE *consults his
list.*) That's all Mrs. Alexander drinks, but she drinks a lot of
them. It's all right for her to get tight, if she wants to—but take
it easy on the rest of them. We want to keep them sober. The
Senator likes Martinis before dinner, then he goes on a steady diet
of Scotch and soda.

SWENSON. Yes, sir.

SPIKE. (*Consulting his list again.*) Now, Mr. Parrish ——

SWENSON. Manhattans for Mr. Parrish, and then rye.

SPIKE. And Mrs. Thorndyke ——?

SWENSON. Mrs. Thorndyke likes a Martini before dinner—very
dry.

SPIKE. All right, give her one. Same for Mrs. Draper. Just have
plenty of Martinis and Manhattans—and Scotch and soda for
Mr. Conover. And remember, Swenson, except for Mrs. Alexander, nobody gets too much to drink—and that goes for Mr. and
Mrs. Matthews, too. (GRANT *enters through arch during last sen-
tence of* SPIKE'S *speech. He is wearing hat and topcoat, and carries
a small wrapped box. He drops hat and box on chair* L. C.)

GRANT. What goes for Mr. and Mrs. Matthews?

SPIKE. I'm straightening Swenson out on the drinks—and nobody's
to get too many. If there's one thing I don't want around here
tonight, it's too much frankness— (GRANT *crosses* L. *behind chairs.*)
—especially from you. I'm thinking of that time you got tight in
San Francisco. We'd been in a hell of a fix if the newspapermen
hadn't gotten drunker. Swenson wanted to know where to put the
place cards. I've got a diagram here.

GRANT. Wait 'til I get Mary. (*He crosses up to stairway* L. *and
then upstairs.*)

SWENSON. There's a Mr. Hardy on the list, sir.

SPIKE. Those labor boys are smart cookies. He doesn't drink anything. (SWENSON *picks up package at* SPIKE'S *feet and goes through
arch* R. *to bar. He leaves package behind bar and exits* R.)

GRANT. Well, make it as soon as you can. I'm late. I should be
changing. (*He comes downstairs, taking off topcoat and putting
it over arm. To* SPIKE.) She'll be here in a minute. (GRANT *crosses
below sofa to fireplace* R., *glancing around room.*)

66

SPIKE. Nervous about tonight?

GRANT. Yes, a little. I feel as though I'm being quietly surrounded.

SPIKE. Take it easy. Let them do the talking.

GRANT. Oh, I'm not making any commitments here tonight. You and Jim and I are meeting over at Kay's after they've gone.

SPIKE. Look, they're going to throw the book at you tonight. That goes for Conover, too. They don't expect you to take it all—it's just as Kay said last night—they'll be willing to compromise.

GRANT. Compromise! Before I got into this, it all seemed so clear and simple. I suppose it does to almost everybody who doesn't have to make the decisions.

SPIKE. Yeah, Mary, for instance.

GRANT. I know now it isn't just black and white—but damn it, where do you draw the line? (*He thinks a moment.*) I know damn well once I got to be President —— (*A pause.*) Well!

SPIKE. I'll drop back about midnight and pick you up and we can talk it out at Kay's.

GRANT. Spike, keep that to yourself—we're supposed to be meeting —— (MARY *enters down stairs. She is in evening dress. There is a lack of warmth between her and* GRANT.)

MARY. (*Crossing to* L. *arm of sofa and sitting.*) Hello, Spike, I'm sorry to get you up here, but I told Grant you had to help seat these people.

SPIKE. I've got a diagram here. (*He shows* MARY *diagram.*) You're here—and Grant's at the other end!

GRANT. (*Sitting on sofa far* R.) Well, if we're going to observe any protocol, Senator Lauterbuck ranks. I think he ought to be on Mary's right.

SPIKE. O. K., and I'll put Mrs. Draper on your right. We're short of women; some of the men will have to sit together.

MARY. Why don't you put Sam Parrish on Grant's left?

GRANT. Don't you want Sam up near you? It'll give you someone to talk to.

MARY. Well, I thought that after what you *didn't* say about profits and high prices in Detroit, you and Sam might want to hold hands under the table.

GRANT. Mary, we've been over that often enough. I *did* talk about profits and high prices in Detroit.

MARY. I wouldn't say about them, Grant. I'd say around them. You did come right out and mention the words once.

GRANT. (*Rising, and speaking with angry finality.*) Mary, I've heard all I want to hear about Detroit.

SPIKE. (*To the rescue.*) Here's a good couple to pair off. Hardy and Mrs. Alexander. He never opens his mouth and she never closes hers. (*He writes them down.*) How about Mrs. Thorndyke up here? (*He points.*)

MARY. How about Mrs. Thorndyke down there? (*She points. Both men look at her.*)

SPIKE. O. K. Then the Judge here, and Jim here. (*He writes and then holds up diagram.*) That looks all right. (*Hands diagram to* MARY.)

GRANT. (*Looking at watch.*) Hell, I've got to get dressed. (*He crosses toward staircase.*)

MARY. Grant, you're looking in on Sonny and Joyce?

GRANT. I certainly am. (*He crosses back to* C.) Mary, I know this dinner isn't going to be much fun for you. It's damn nice of you to do it for me. I appreciate it.

MARY. (*Not facing* GRANT.) Nonsense, Grant. I hope it's everything you want it to be. I'll do my best. Just to show you how serious I am about it, I'm not even going to have a cocktail.

GRANT. I'm going light myself. (*He starts off* L., *then notices his hat and box on chair.*) Oh, Mary, I almost forgot. This is for tonight. (*He hands her box and hurries off.* MARY *rises and crosses to* C. *She watches* GRANT *exit.*)

MARY. (*Almost to herself.*) I didn't think he even remembered it!

SPIKE. Remembered what?

MARY. Today's our wedding anniversary. Excuse me, Spike! (*She takes off wrapping eagerly, removing a box of cigars.*) My error! (*JENNY enters from* R. *arch.*) Jenny!

JENNY. (*Crossing to* MARY.) Yes, Madam?

MARY. Here's the table diagram. Will you take care of the place cards? And these cigars?

JENNY. (*Taking both diagram and cigars.*) Very good, Madam. (*JENNY exits* U. L. C. *into back hall.*)

SPIKE. (*With forced gaiety.*) Those cigars are Benson and Hedges, the only brand Conover smokes. Don't tell me Grant doesn't know how to play politics!

MARY. Oh, I know he plays politics! I've found that out! (*In unhappy puzzlement.*) I wish I knew why he changed his speech in Detroit!

68

SPIKE. (*Casually.*) Jim talked to him, didn't he? Warned him not to say anything that would cost us any campaign contributions.

MARY. (*Crossing to* L. *end of sofa.*) No, Spike, it wasn't for money. So if you do know you won't tell me. You're not on my team. And I've often wondered why. You know, Spike, you've got a very wide streak of decency.

SPIKE. Yes, if I don't watch it, it gets in my way. (*Seriously.*) Look, Mary, I'll pull every trick I know to get Grant in the White House, but once he's there and I'm back on the newspaper, I'll be on the same team with you; and if Grant isn't in there pitching for the people, I'll burn his pants off!

MARY. I'll light the matches for you.

SPIKE. (*Rising.*) But don't start any bonfires here tonight. (JENNY *crosses hall, on her way to outer door.*) These educated apes that are coming here—Grant can't be nominated without their support, and in the election they can deliver a lot of votes.

MARY. How can you deliver the votes of a free people?

SPIKE. Don't kid yourself, Mary. Lazy people, ignorant people and prejudiced people are not free. (*We hear the voice of* JUDGE ALEXANDER *offstage.*)

ALEXANDER. (*Off.*) Is Mrs. Matthews in?

JENNY. (*Off.*) This way, sir.

SPIKE. (*Picking up ashtray and putting it on the table,* R.) Somebody's here. I'd better run. I'll be back in time to help you sweep them out.

MARY. Wait until whoever this is comes in, will you, Spike? I don't know them all. (JUDGE JEFFERSON DAVIS ALEXANDER *and* MRS. LULUBELLE ALEXANDER *enter. She is still wearing her wrap, which she hands to* JENNY *who exits with it to room down* L. *The* ALEXANDERS *are from the deep South. He is tall and lean. She is short and plump.*)

SPIKE. (*Holding out his hand.*) Hello, Judge. I'm Spike Mac-Manus. Remember me?

ALEXANDER. (*Expansively, crossing to shake hands with* SPIKE.) Indeed I do. It's a great pleasure to see you again, sir! This is Mrs. Alexander. (MRS. LULUBELLE ALEXANDER *is standing* L. *of* JUDGE.)

SPIKE. How do you do. Mrs. Matthews, this is Judge Alexander and Mrs. Alexander. (SPIKE *crosses* L. *to back of chair.*)

MARY. (*Holding out her hand.*) How do you do, Judge Alexander?

ALEXANDER. (*Crossing to* MARY *and shaking hands.*) It's an honor to be here, Mrs. Matthews.

MARY. (*To* LULUBELLE.) I'm especially glad you could come, Mrs. Alexander. We women are going to be outnumbered here tonight.

LULUBELLE. That's nothing new to me, Mrs. Matthews. When I go to dinner with the Judge's Republican friends I'm always outnumbered. I make it a point to tell my hostess right off that while Jeff's a Republican, I'm a Democrat. But you can speak freely. You Republicans can't say anything about the Administration mean enough for us Democrats down South.

SPIKE. I'll leave you my proxy, Mrs. Alexander. I've got to run along. Good night. Good night, Mary. Good night, Judge.

ALEXANDER. (*Heartily.*) It's been very pleasant seeing you again, sir! Good night! (SPIKE *exits waving.* *To* MARY.) Who is he? (JENNY *enters from room* L. *and exits arch* L. *upstage.*)

MARY. A newspaperman. He's been helping my husband. Won't you sit down? (LULUBELLE *crosses and sits in chair* L. C.) Mr. Matthews will be down in a minute.

ALEXANDER. Mrs. Alexander and I are certainly looking forward to meeting him. (SWENSON *enters from behind* L. *arch and stands* L. *of* ALEXANDER.)

MARY. You must be looking forward to a cocktail, too?

LULUBELLE. Frankly, I'm looking forward to both.

SWENSON. (*To* ALEXANDER.) Bourbon, sir?

ALEXANDER. You read my mind.

LULUBELLE. He can't read my mind.

SWENSON. (*Turning to* LULUBELLE.) A Sazarac, I believe?

ALEXANDER. Lulubelle—your reputation's getting too far north.

MARY. Swenson, can you make a Sazarac?

SWENSON. I think so, ma'am.

LULUBELLE. If he just thinks so, Jeff, you'd better mix that Sazarac.

ALEXANDER. Yes, honey.

MARY. (*Indicating.*) The bar's right over there.

SWENSON. This way, sir. (*He crosses behind* ALEXANDER *and leads him to bar and starts showing him where liquor and glasses can be found.*)

MARY. (*Crossing to* LULUBELLE.) Do you get up North often?

LULUBELLE. Being a Republican down South, the Judge only gets

70

important every four years—around Convention time. Jim Conover getting him way up here this early must mean they're pretty
serious about running your husband for President, which I hope
they don't.

MARY. Really?

LULUBELLE. Yes, you seem like such a nice woman. Politics is
too good an excuse for a man to neglect his wife.

MARY. Well, at least if you're neglected tonight—you and I can
be neglected together. (*She hears voices off* L., *and crosses up* C.
JENNY *ushers in* MRS. DRAPER *and* JIM CONOVER. JENNY *takes*
MRS. DRAPER'S *wrap and exits into room* L.)

CONOVER. (*Crossing to* MARY.) Hello, Mary. This is Mrs. Draper,
Mrs. Matthews. (*He crosses to* LULUBELLE.) Hello, Lulubelle,
where's the Judge?

MRS. DRAPER. (*Crossing to*
MARY *and shaking hands.*) I've
been so eager to meet you and
your husband.

MARY. It's so nice that you
could come. Do you know Mrs.
Alexander? (MRS. DRAPER
crosses to LULUBELLE.)

CONOVER. Mrs. Matthews, this
is Bill Hardy. (HARDY *crosses
to* MARY *and shakes hands.*)

MARY. Hello, Mr. Hardy.

HARDY. Nobody told me not to
dress.

CONOVER. My fault, Bill. I
slipped up on that.

MARY. I'm glad you did dress.
Men are getting all too lazy
about dressing.

CONOVER. Isn't that what you're
after, Bill? Put evening clothes
on labor and let the rest of us
go without? Come on and have
a drink. (SENATOR *enters.* CON-
OVER *points out bar to* HARDY.

LULUBELLE. Mixing me a drink.

CONOVER. Well, this is where I
went out. (HARDY *enters.* CON-
OVER *crosses to bar* R.) Hello,
Judge!

ALEXANDER. (*From bar.*) Hello,
Jim!

MRS. DRAPER. (*To* LULU-
BELLE.) You're Judge Alexan-
der's wife. I met you in
Chicago.

LULUBELLE. Oh, yes, at the
Convention. I was so glad to
get back down South away from
that heat. (MRS. DRAPER *crosses
to sofa* R. *and sits down.*)
SWENSON *has entered from bar
with another tray of drinks.*)

71

SENATOR *steps up.*) Oh, Mary, this is Senator Lauterback.

SENATOR. (*Shaking hands with* MARY.) Wanted to meet you ever since you made that trip with your husband. You were just as big a hit as he was. He talks well but you're prettier.

CONOVER. Mr. Matthews will be down in a minute, Senator. Have a drink. (SENATOR *turns up to bar and takes cocktail off tray as* SWENSON *passes him.*)

MARY. (*Crossing below* CONOVER *to* U. C., *as* SWENSON *comes up with tray of drinks.*) You want a highball, don't you, Jim?

CONOVER. Well, we've just come from a little caucus in my room at the hotel. We did some drinking there. Oh, all right. (*He takes a highball from tray.* SWENSON *turns to offer drink to* MARY.)

MARY. No, thank you, Swenson. I'm not taking anything to drink tonight. (SWENSON *serves drink to* MRS. DRAPER. KAY THORNDYKE *enters and stands in arch.* MARY *turns and sees her.*) Hello, Kay.

KAY. Hello, Mary. (KAY *walks forward with outstretched hand.*) You're looking very pretty tonight.

MARY. (*Taking Martini from tray and handing it to* KAY.) You're just in time for a cocktail. (SWENSON *returns to bar to reload tray with prepared drinks on* L. *end of bar out of sight.*) Do you know everyone here? (KAY *and* MARY *move down* C.)

KAY. I know Mrs. Draper. (*The* JUDGE *has entered from bar with* LULUBELLE'S *Sazarac, which he hands to her.*)

MARY. Mrs. Alexander, this is Mrs. Thorndyke—and Judge Alexander. (CONOVER *has crossed above sofa and* D. R.)

KAY. How do you do?

LULUBELLE. Hello, Mrs. Thorndyke. (LULUBELLE *starts her drinking.*)

ALEXANDER. (*Above table* L.) Mrs. Thorndyke, I'm very pleased to meet you. I was raised in the old tradition of the South, where it was looked down on for a woman to go into anything like newspaper business. (*Crosses to* KAY.) But no gentleman of the South could deny as attractive a woman as you your outstanding suc-

72

cess. Which reminds me of a story.—A number of years ago when I was a small boy ——

LULUBELLE. Jeff, this is the best Sazarac I ever had in my life. Mix me another one right away!

ALEXANDER. Yes, honey. (*He crosses to bar.*)

MRS. DRAPER. Kay, after you left, Jim and I went into the situation in Chicago. (*Turns to* CONOVER.) Jim, tell her what you said.

KAY. Oh, Grace, let's take time out of politics for a little drinking. (*To* MARY.) You're in for a bad evening, Mary.

MARY. Oh, no! Politics is new to me, but I'm very interested.

CONOVER. (*Amiably, but sardonically.*) You've got the " very " in the wrong place, Mary. Interested, but very new.

MARY. (*To others, smiling.*) Mr. Conover means I haven't lost my amateur standing.

CONOVER. You're learning—I hope!

MARY. (*Crossing to* L. *end sofa.*) That's a dangerous hope, Jim. You politicians have stayed professionals because the voters have remained amateurs. (SAM PARRISH *enters* L. *arch.* MARY *crosses to* C.)

SAM. Hello, everybody! Late as usual! Had a hell of a day! (*Crossing to* MARY *at* C.) How's my sweetheart?

MARY. Hello, Sam. (SAM *kisses her.* KAY *crosses* R. *above sofa.*)

SAM. That's for Hilda! (*He kisses her again.*) That's for me! (*Hearing* SAM, HARDY *and the* SENATOR *drift into room* R. *of* MARY.) Jim, I won't get down to Washington until afternoon. How about dinner instead of lunch?

CONOVER. That suits me even better.

SENATOR. (R. *of* MARY.) Hello, Sam.

SAM. (*Crossing to* SENATOR *and shaking hands.*) Senator! You'll be glad to hear I'm starting a back-to-the-farm movement. Just closed down two plants. (HARDY *steps into view from behind* SENATOR.) Oh, hello, Bill! Shouldn't have said that in front of you! (*Turns to* MARY.) Mary, do I have to sit down with Labor again tonight? Where's Grant?

MARY. He'll be down any minute.

MRS. DRAPER. Hello, Sam!

SAM. Hello, Grace!

MARY. Do you know Mrs. Alexander? Mr. Parrish.

SAM. (*Crossing to* R. *of* LULUBELLE.) How are you, Mrs. Alexander?

MARY. And have you met Mrs. Thorndyke?

KAY. (*Crossing* D. S. *to front of sofa.*) Oh, yes, we know each other. Nice seeing you again, Mr. Parrish.

SAM. (*To* KAY.) Where did you get to that night? I looked all over the banquet hall for you. (*There is an embarrassed pause.*)

KAY. I didn't go to the banquet.

CONOVER. (*To the rescue.*) Say, how's Hilda?

SAM. She's fine now. Mrs. Thorndyke, I thought that was why you were in Detroit—to hear Grant's speech.

MARY. (*Standing* L. *end of sofa. To* KAY.) Were you in Detroit when we were there, Kay?

SAM. Yes, you must have seen her, Mary. She was on her way to your suite. I'd just left you, remember?

MARY. I didn't see Mrs. Thorndyke in Detroit. (*To* KAY.) Oh, you must have dropped in to talk to Grant about profits and high prices?

SAM. What Grant said about profits and high prices in his speech that night was all right. You couldn't argue with it.

MARY. (*Still looking at* KAY.) Well, I think you can thank Mrs. Thorndyke for that.

CONOVER. (*Interrupting and crossing* C. *to* SAM.) Sam, did you get that finance report I sent you?

SAM. Yes, and it's a damn bad job. I've made you a whole new list. (*He searches through his pockets.* JUDGE *enters from bar with two Sazaracs and crosses to* LULUBELLE.)

KAY. (*To* MRS. DRAPER.) Grace, I'm having another cocktail.

MRS. DRAPER. I'll have one, too. (*They both cross up* R. *of sofa to bar.*)

MARY. (*Turning to* CONOVER.) Well, Jim, you hoped I'd learn. I'm learning.

SAM. Left it in my overcoat. I'll get it. (*Starts out and sees* JUDGE.) Hello, Judge! You drinking with both hands now?

ALEXANDER. Hello, Sam! These aren't for me. (SAM *exits into hall. To* LULUBELLE, *placing drinks on table.*) Honey, I want to talk to some of these people, so I brought you two of them. (CONOVER *crosses up* R. *toward bar.*)

LULUBELLE. Thank you, Jeff. (*She takes fresh drink.*)

MARY. (*Crossing to* R. *of* LULUBELLE.) Judge, I'll have one of those. (JUDGE *hands her a drink.*)

74

CONOVER. (*Concerned.*) Mary, those are pretty powerful. I thought you weren't drinking anything tonight?

MARY. I thought if we are going to have high tariffs and high prices, I'd get a little high myself.

LULUBELLE. Jeff, make another one for me right away.

ALEXANDER. Yes, honey. (*He starts for bar.*)

MARY. H'm-m, I like these. Judge, would you make another one for me, too? (MARY *crosses down* L. *and sits chair* L. JUDGE *starts toward bar.* GRANT *comes down the stairs into the arch as* SAM *enters from* L. *with a sheaf of papers in his hand.* JUDGE *crosses down to* C. *of sofa* R.)

SAM. Grant!

GRANT. Hello, Sam! (*They shake hands and enter together.* CON-OVER *has crossed* U. C.)

SAM. All I've got to decide tonight is whether we're going to run you for a third term.

CONOVER. How're you, Grant? You certainly took time to pretty yourself up.

GRANT. Was it successful? Sorry I'm late.

ALEXANDER. Mr. Matthews, I'm Judge Alexander.

GRANT. (*With a gesture.*) Not guilty! (*He crosses to* JUDGE *and shakes hands.* SAM *sits chair* U. C. CONOVER *goes into conference with* SAM.)

ALEXANDER. Sir, I reject your plea. I'm sentencing you to four years in the White House.

GRANT. (*Laughing.*) You're taking Jim Conover more seriously than I am. (MARY *and* LULUBELLE *drink steadily.*)

ALEXANDER. Mr. Conover's a man to be taken seriously. Due to his efforts I almost had the honor of being the last man appointed to public office by Herbert Hoover. But the Federal Judge we expected to die held on a few days and the first thing we knew Mr. Roosevelt was in office. So I'm still on the State bench. However, my term expires in 1948. So ——

LULUBELLE. Jeff!

ALEXANDER. Yes, honey?

LULUBELLE. I'm going to be needing my other drink.

MARY. Grant, this is Mrs. Alexander. (GRANT *crosses and shakes hands with* LULUBELLE. JUDGE *exits to bar.*)

GRANT. How do you do, Mrs. Alexander?

LULUBELLE. (*To* MARY.) Handsome, isn't he? (*Looking at*

GRANT.) He's the first good reason I've ever seen for voting Republican. I warned your wife I was a Democrat.

GRANT. Some of my best friends are Democrats.

LULUBELLE. Well, you know us Southerners. We vote Democratic at home, but we've got an awfully good Republican record in Congress. (KAY, MRS. DRAPER, HARDY *and* SENATOR *come in from bar.* SWENSON *arrives at this moment from bar at* GRANT'S *side with a tray of drinks.* GRANT *takes a martini and turns to* MARY.)

GRANT. Cocktail, Mary? Oh, you're not drinking anything, are you?

MARY. (*Holding glass aloft.*) Yes! Sazaracs!

GRANT. (*Surprised.*) Oh? (KAY *crosses to front of sofa.* MRS. DRAPER *crosses back of sofa to* L. *of it.* HARDY *follows* KAY. SENATOR *stays at rear* R. *end sofa.*)

KAY. Hello, Grant! (GRANT *turns and crosses to her.*)

GRANT. Oh, hello, Kay! Nice seeing you again. (*They shake hands.*)

KAY. This is Bill Hardy.

GRANT. Glad you're here, Mr. Hardy.

HARDY. Nobody told me not to dress. (HARDY *shakes hands and turns petulantly to fireplace.*)

KAY. And this is Grace Draper. (GRANT *turns and shakes hands.*)

GRANT. (*To* MRS. DRAPER.) I've been looking forward to meeting you, Mrs. Draper. You're on the National Committee, I believe?

KAY. And they're going to run Mrs. Draper for Congress.

GRANT. Fine! I always say a woman's place is in the House.

SENATOR. (*Crossing down to* R. *of* KAY.) Just so they stay out of the Senate. How are you, Mr. Matthews? I'm Senator Lauterback. (*They shake hands across* KAY.)

GRANT. Oh, of course. (CONOVER *comes down and joins group* C.)

SENATOR. We met before, in a manner of speaking. Remember you testified before my Committee. You made a very strong impression on us.

GRANT. (*Amused.*) Well, I never would have guessed it from the Committee's report. (SWENSON *starts from bar with tray of drinks.*)

CONOVER. The Senator was just telling me about that, Grant. He can give you the inside on it. I think you'll find it very interesting. (CONOVER *crosses back up* C. SWENSON *approaches the group around* GRANT *with a tray of drinks.*)

GRANT. Senator, we'll have to go into that later. I'd like to hear about it. (*To* MRS. DRAPER.) Another cocktail, Mrs. Draper?

MRS. DRAPER. Thank you. They're very good. (*She takes one.*)

GRANT. (*To* KAY.) How about you, Kay?

KAY. No, two's my limit.

GRANT. (*To* SENATOR.) How about you, Senator? Or would you rather have a highball?

SENATOR. No, I'll stick to these. (*He takes one.*) And very good, too!

GRANT. (*To* HARDY.) Want that refreshed, Mr. Hardy?

HARDY. No, you can drink just so much Coca-Cola.

LULUBELLE. (*To* MARY, *pointing.*) You see, that's what happens when your husband gets into politics. You just sit off in a corner.

MARY. We have each other for company tonight, and it gives us time to attend to our drinking. (*She finishes her Sazarac just as the* JUDGE *arrives with two more. Both women take fresh drinks.*)

LULUBELLE. Just in time, Jeff. Fix us some more, right away.

ALEXANDER. Honey, there are a lot of things I want to talk to Mr. Matthews about.

LULUBELLE. Mix the drinks before you start talkin', Jeff; you know how I hate to interrupt you. (*JUDGE hurries back to bar, muttering.*)

ALEXANDER. Yes, honey.

(SWENSON *returns to bar, then disappears into dining-room.*)

KAY. (*To* SENATOR.) I'm glad you mentioned that, Senator. (*To* GRANT.) Grant, the Senator and Mrs. Draper are very interested in what you plan to say at the Foreign Policy Association Thursday night.

GRANT. (*To* MRS. DRAPER.) Yes, Thursday's the night I settle world affairs.

KAY. Grace is the Party's expert on the foreign vote.

MRS. DRAPER. I think the election in '48 will turn on it.

KAY. (*To* GRANT.) Take the Italians, for instance.

MRS. DRAPER. (*Cutting in.*) Yes, if we called their attention to it the Italians over here could be made very unhappy about the peace terms.

KAY. Truman has to take responsibility for the peace terms. So you see, Grant, it's not going to be hard to appeal to the Italian vote.

GRANT. Just how do you propose to go about that?

77

KAY. It's very simple. We just have to demand justice for Italy. (MARY, *who has been listening to this, speaks up.*)

MARY. If you favor Italy, won't that lose you the Abyssinian vote?

MRS. DRAPER. (*Turning to* MARY.) Mrs. Matthews, there isn't any Abyssinian vote.

MARY. Good! We don't have to worry about justice for the Abyssinians. (MARY *takes a drink.*)

KAY. (*Turning to* GRANT.) Grant, in this next election Mrs. Draper feels the Polish vote is the most important.

MRS. DRAPER. (*To* GRANT.) Indeed I do! Now in your speech Thursday night you should come out for the reopening of the whole Polish question.—Denounce their last election and demand we break off diplomatic relations.

KAY. Any strong stand, Grant, would clinch the Polish vote.

MARY. I thought the Poles voted in Poland?

KAY. (*To* MARY.) We're talking about Polish-Americans.

MARY. Oh, can you be both?

SAM. (*Looking up from his papers.*) Mary, I love you, but this is practical politics, and you're way out over your head.

MARY. (*To* SAM.) Well, if they're Americans I should think you'd ask them to vote as Americans, not as Poles!

GRANT. (*Too heartily.*) Mary, I think we could all use some more hors d'oeuvres. (MARY *rises and crosses to bell in* L. *wall* U. S. *of door.*)

KAY. (*To* MRS. DRAPER.) Take the Greek situation, for instance . . .

MARY. (*Turning back toward group.*) Is this what's called power politics?

SENATOR. (*Crossing to* R. *of* LULUBELLE'S *chair.*) Mrs. Matthews, power politics is what they play in Europe. (KAY *crosses to sit on ottoman* R. MRS. DRAPER *sits on sofa.*)

MARY. (*Crossing back to her chair.*) It seems to me we're beginning to play it right here. Let's disunite the United Nations and keep America safe for the Republicans. (*She sits.* JUDGE *comes out of the bar with a tray holding four Sazaracs. He crosses to table* L. *of* LULUBELLE.)

ALEXANDER. Doggone it, I'm missing out on everything. (*Places tray on table and addresses* LULUBELLE.) Honey, I made you four this time. I'm starved for some good Republican talk. (JENNY

78

enters from L. *arch in answer to bell.* MARY *and* LULUBELLE *each take a fresh Sazarac.*)

GRANT. Jenny, some hors d'oeuvres, please. (JENNY *gets tray on table at foot of stairs and passes it during the following to* MARY *and* LULUBELLE, *crosses to group at sofa above, then exits.*)

LULUBELLE. (*Raising her glass to* MARY.) More power to you!

MARY. Thanks! They're full of it, aren't they? (MARY *starts on her third Sazarac.*)

ALEXANDER. (*Crossing to* GRANT L. *of sofa.*) Mr. Matthews, if I may say so, I think you are the hope of the new South.

SENATOR. Here we go again! The Judge is going to promise that we'll break the solid South.

ALEXANDER. Senator, you don't understand the conditions down there.

SENATOR. All I have to say is that when a State votes the same way for one hundred years, it's a reflection on the intelligence of the electorate. (*Turns to* MARY.) Don't you agree with me, Mrs. Matthews?

MARY. I'm from Vermont. (*She drinks.* JUDGE *crosses to* SENATOR *and pats him on shoulder, then exits to bar, laughing.*)

SENATOR. That's not the same thing. Vermont's always been a good sound Republican state. (*Crosses to* GRANT.) Mr. Matthews, in your speech Thursday I know you have to tie up world peace with tariff reductions, and we realize industry has to make some sacrifices along that line ——

SAM. (*Calling out from table and rising.*) Oh, industry has to make the sacrifices!

SENATOR. But I think you'll have to reassure the American farmer that he won't be forced to compete with Canadian wheat and Danish butter and Australian wool.

GRANT. Senator, there's a direct connection between world trade and world peace.

KAY. Yes, but, Grant, the farmer has a special case.

SENATOR. And twenty million votes.

GRANT. Senator, I want you to talk to me very, very frankly and very fully, and give me all the information you can—but please don't expect me to make any decisions here tonight.

MARY. That's the way Grant works. He likes to listen to people before he makes any decish—(*She looks at drink, then places it carefully on table.*)—before he *decides* anything.

SAM. (*Crossing down to group* C.) I thought we were going to talk turkey tonight. If I'm going to raise this money, I've got to take word back to Detroit how Grant stands on certain issues.

CONOVER. (*Following* SAM *down to* C.) After you've gone, Grant and I are going to hold a caucus. We'll have word for all of you tomorrow.

SENATOR. (*To* SAM.) Sam, Mr. Matthews' strength is with big business. Why should they be worried about him?

SAM. You know what we're worried about. Are we going to be in for a lot of government competition, or is this country going to be put back in the hands of private enterprise? (SWENSON *enters from arch* L. *and crosses to* L. C.)

MARY. (*Rising.*) Oh, Grant believes in private enterprise. (*She stares across at* KAY.) Doesn't he, Kay?

SWENSON. Dinner is served, ma'am. (SWENSON *exits through arch* R.)

GRANT. Dinner. Good! Take your cocktails with you if you haven't finished. (*He crosses to* C.) Mary! (*Group starts for bar alcove, ad libbing as they go.* MARY *puts down her empty cocktail glass and starts for dining room.* LULUBELLE *has finished her Sazarac and picks up another to take with her.*)

MARY. (*Crossing to arch* R.) Find your own place cards. I hope some of you men don't mind sitting together? There aren't enough women to go around. (MARY *leads way, followed by* MRS. DRAPER *and* LULUBELLE, *then* HARDY, ALEXANDER, SAM, SENATOR *and* CONOVER. KAY *rises from ottoman and crosses* L. *of* GRANT, *who is at end of procession* U. C.)

KAY. (*With cold anger.*) Grant, Mary's tight. Is there any way you can talk to her?—Do something with her?

GRANT. (*Worried.*) What happened?

KAY. It was Sam. The minute he walked into the room he —— (MARY *enters from dining-room, speaking back over her shoulder.*)

MARY. Find your place cards, everyone. I forgot my—(*She turns and sees* GRANT *and* KAY.)—cocktail. (KAY *brushes past her to dining-room.*)

GRANT. Mary, I'm depending on you to help me tonight.

MARY. (*Crossing to table* L.) I'm afraid I interrupted you and Kay before she had a chance to tell you what you think. (*She picks up drink from table without leaning over.*)

GRANT. (*Crossing down to* R. *of* MARY.) Leave that drink here, and get some food into you as soon as you can!

MARY. (*Challengingly.*) Well, it seems to me you're getting a little " belligerel."

GRANT. Mary, I'm on a spot here tonight. We both are. We have to be ready to do some quick thinking.

MARY. (*Starting for exit* U. R.) Don't worry about me. (*She stops* C. *and looks back at* GRANT.) I'm a very thick quinker. (MARY *starts for dining-room, walking with careful deliberation.* GRANT *starts to follow.*)

CURTAIN

ACT III

SCENE 2

The same. An hour later.

DISCOVERED AT RISE: MARY *and* LULUBELLE *are seated down* L. MARY, *in* R. *chair, is drinking coffee with a certain desperation. On the table between them is* LULU-BELLE'S *demitasse, untouched.* LULUBELLE *is at work on a Sazarac.* MARY *finishes her coffee, puts it down on table and notices* LULUBELLE'S *full cup. She eyes it for a second, and then speaks to* LULUBELLE.

MARY. You haven't touched your coffee.

LULUBELLE. Never use it. Keeps me awake nights.

MARY. (*Picking up cup.*) Do you mind? (*She pushes her own cup to* LULUBELLE'S *place.*)

LULUBELLE. Help yourself, honey. (MARY *starts on* LULUBELLE'S *coffee.* LULUBELLE *is sipping her highball as though her immediate memories gave her some amusement.* SWENSON *appears with a coffee pot on a tray. He approaches the empty cup which* MARY *has put down.*)

SWENSON. (*To* LULUBELLE.) More coffee, ma'am?

MARY. (*Turning slightly.*) Yes, Swenson. (*He fills empty cup, then turns to* MARY.)

SWENSON. Coffee, madam?

MARY. Yes, please. (*She quickly finishes coffee in her cup, then*

81

holds it out for refill.) Be sure everyone in the dining-room is taken care of. And did you remember Mr. Conover's cigars?

SWENSON. Yes, madam. (SWENSON *starts for bar alcove.* MRS. DRAPER *enters. He allows her to pass and then exits* R. MRS. DRAPER *heads for room* L. *but stops* C. *and points toward it.*)

MRS. DRAPER. Am I right? (*She points to bedroom* L. MARY *nods, giving her the best smile she can muster.* MRS. DRAPER *hurries into room* L., *closing door.*)

LULUBELLE. You know, I thought she spoke to you real friendly.

MARY. Shouldn't she have? What did I say to her?

LULUBELLE. I can't quite remember, honey, but it was followed by one of the loudest silences I've ever heard. (MARY *suffers and gulps coffee,* LULUBELLE *takes a drink of highball.*)

MARY. I can't remember anything that happened before the salad.

LULUBELLE. You missed the best part. You certainly were whamming away at them. You picked them off one by one—like settin' birds. I haven't enjoyed myself so much since Huey Long died. (*She takes another drink.*)

MARY. (*Taking another gulp of coffee.*) Can you remember any of the things I said?

LULUBELLE. (*Thinking.*) Now let me see—what was it you said to the Senator? I kept wishing I had a pencil so I could write 'em down. It may come back to me later. That was the time Sam Parrish had the choking spell. You remember that, don't you?

MARY. (*Disconsolately.*) No. (*Another gulp of coffee.*)

LULUBELLE. Oh, he had to leave the table. Then when he came back you started on him.

MARY. Oh, dear! (*She puts her empty cup down and takes up* LULUBELLE'S *full one.*)

LULUBELLE. It was something personal that I couldn't rightly follow. Your husband got it. That's when he knocked over his wine. My!—and that looked like an expensive dress Mrs. Thorndyke is wearing. (MARY *comes out of coffee cup with broad smile and turns to* LULUBELLE.) I don't think she likes you, honey. She was the only one that tried to get back at you, but you took care of her.

MARY. What were they talking about?

LULUBELLE. It was kinda hard to keep track of it, because every time you said something they changed the subject. (MARY *suffers.*) After we've gone, you'd better make up to your husband.

82

I don't think he thought that talk about the thermometer was very funny.

MARY. Thermometer? What thermometer?

LULUBELLE. Oh, you just kept bedevilling him to take his temperature.

MARY. Why?

LULUBELLE. Well, you said he was getting another one of his attacks of gallopin' self-importance. (MARY *winces*.) I remember that one! I'm saving that one up to use on Jeff! (JENNY *crosses back of arch to outer door.* LULUBELLE *finishes her drink.*)

MARY. I certainly picked a good day for this. (*Turns to* LULUBELLE.) It's our wedding anniversary.

LULUBELLE. (*Thoughtfully.*) Well, honey, this is one anniversary you'll both always remember! (SWENSON *enters from dining-room with a tray holding a silver coffee pot and* LULUBELLE'S *bourbon. Helping herself to drink from tray.*) Oh, thank you!

SWENSON. (*Pouring coffee for* MARY.) Shall I leave this here?

MARY. Yes, please. Thanks, Swenson. (*He puts tray on table.* SPIKE *enters through arch.* JENNY *is seen crossing* R.)

SPIKE. (*Crossing to* D. C.) Hello, there! How's everything going?

MARY. Just daisy. (SWENSON *picks up* LULUBELLE'S *empty glass and starts to exit to arch* L.)

SPIKE. (*To* SWENSON.) Will you tell Mr. Matthews I'm here? (SWENSON *bows and exits.*)

MARY. They're still in the dining-room, talking politics.

SPIKE. Did they get too much for you?

MARY. I got too much for them.

SPIKE. (*Concerned.*) Oh-oh!

MARY. And don't ask for a copy of my speech. No matter what they tell you, I've been misquoted. (GRANT *appears in ach* R.)

GRANT. Hello, Spike, come on in! You know everybody.

SPIKE. How's it going? (*He crosses to* GRANT R.)

GRANT. I don't know.

SPIKE. If it's a smoke-filled room, I can tell you—you're nominated. (SPIKE *exits into dining-room.* GRANT *looks at his watch. He speaks in* MARY'S *general direction.*)

GRANT. I didn't know it was that late. Spike came to get Jim and me. We're going over to Jim's hotel afterwards for a post-mortem. Swenson taking care of you, Mrs. Alexander?

LULUBELLE. Yes, thank you. We're having a good time in here.

GRANT. We're having a good time in there—now. (GRANT *exits into dining-room.* MARY *hastily drinks more coffee.*)

LULUBELLE. You blame it all on me, honey. You tell him I started you drinking those Sazaracs.

MARY. (*Painfully.*) What's in those buzz bombs? (MRS. DRAPER *enters from room* L. *to* C.)

LULUBELLE. Mrs. Draper, you've given me an idea. (*She rises and exits into room* L.)

MARY. (*To* MRS. DRAPER.) Won't you sit down and have a drink with us?

MRS. DRAPER. I have to catch a train. I'm just going back to say my good nights. (CONOVER *enters from bar alcove.*)

CONOVER. (*Crossing down to* C.) Oh, Grace, I was afraid you'd gone. The talk has swung around to your territory. They need some information.

MRS. DRAPER. (*Crossing to alcove* R.) I can only stay a couple of minutes. (*She exits.*)

CONOVER. (*To* MARY.) Can I get you a drink?

MARY. Not until about 1952.

CONOVER. Oh, I forgot to tell you. There's been a shake-up in my secret service. I'll prove it to you. The Colonel, who used to be a Major, is now a General.

MARY. Really?

CONOVER. He must be quite a guy.

MARY. He is.

CONOVER. Better keep in touch with him. Send him congratulations.

MARY. No, Jim. When he was a major—I admit he was a major interest. (*Putting cup on table.*) But now, although he's a general, he's just a general interest. (CONOVER *studies* MARY *for a minute.*)

CONOVER. Mary, you once spoke of a spanking as an indication of deep affection. There were some moments tonight when I could have turned you over my knee, but there wouldn't have been any affection in it.

MARY. All right, Jim. I'll agree I've behaved badly as a hostess. I'm not proud of my bad manners. But I'll bet you I'd be proud of what I said—if I could remember what I said.

CONOVER. (*Amused in spite of himself.*) You did let go some beauts.

MARY. Well, I think they're all stupid, selfish people.

84

CONOVER. I'd like to tell you how stupid I think you are. (*He crosses to her chair.*) Mary, I think it's time YOU were a little selfish, *and* a little intelligent. There's such a thing as enlightened self-interest, you know. Why should you be stupid, just because Kay's being stupid?

MARY. Jim, that's one thing even I can't say about Kay—she's not stupid.

CONOVER. Isn't she? She's in there now doing her damnedest to get Grant into the White House. And the White House is the one place where she can't be with him. She can't follow him there, Mary. Have you ever thought of that?

MARY. No, I hadn't.

CONOVER. Well, isn't it a little unintelligent of you to do anything to stop Grant from getting there? If he doesn't become President, I'm not so sure what's going to happen between you and him. But if he is elected—then you'll be the First Lady—in more ways than one.

MARY. That doesn't necessarily follow.

CONOVER. I think it does—and I'll tell you why. I know how you feel toward Grant. You've never bothered to conceal it from me.

MARY. (*Looking down at her lap.*) Okay. So I love him.

CONOVER. Mary, when I saw you and Grant in Detroit—before he spoke that night—there were two people in love. Maybe Grant hadn't said so—maybe Grant hadn't shown it in those little ways you were looking for—but if you had had another month alone together, you know what would have happened.

MARY. I think you're wrong, Jim.

CONOVER. No, my dear, what he feels toward you goes pretty deep—and I'll tell you how he gives himself away. It's in his respect for your opinion—for what you think.

MARY. Don't try to kid me, Jim. We both know what happened to Grant's speech in Detroit.

CONOVER. (*Sitting arm of chair.*) Well, here's something you don't know—how unhappy Grant is about that. He's good and sore at himself and I know in my bones that some day what he thinks about high prices and profits—and what you think—is going to pop right out in the middle of a speech. I'm only praying that it doesn't happen before the nomination, and you'd better say a prayer, too.

MARY. But I want him to say it.

CONOVER. No, Mary, not before the nomination. That's playing Kay's game. (SPIKE *enters arch* R.)

SPIKE. Jim, can you come back in here? They're just breaking up.

CONOVER. I'll be there in a minute. (SPIKE *exits.* CONOVER *turns back to* MARY.) Mary, use your head. You can keep Grant from being President, but if you do, you're going to lose him. (CONOVER *rises to* R. *of* MARY.) Will you do something for me before I go tonight?

MARY. What?

CONOVER. I'd like to hear you say something to Grant that would let him know that if he does come our way just a little, you wouldn't make life miserable for him. (MARY *is silent.*) You're not the only one to be considered, Mary. Think of your children. That's a pretty good heritage—to be able to say, " My father was President of the United States."

MARY. Thanks, Jim. You're better than black coffee. You'd better get back in there.

CONOVER. (*Crossing* R.) Oh, I'll hear it all later.

MARY. Oh, yes, Grant and Spike are going over to your hotel with you.

CONOVER. (*Stopping at arch.*) No, Mary, we're going over to Mrs. Thorndyke's. (*He stands for a minute watching* MARY, *who slowly turns and stares at him, then he exits through arch* R. MARY *thinks a few seconds, then rises and crosses in a determined manner* R., *when she hears* VOICES *offstage and stops back of sofa.*)

MRS. DRAPER. Good night, everybody! (*She enters with* GRANT *and* HARDY. CONOVER *and* SENATOR *enter and stand near bar.*) I'm sorry I have to run. I'm afraid I broke up the party.

GRANT. I'm sure you'll have time to get your train.

MRS. DRAPER. (*Crossing to* L. *door.*) I have to stop at the hotel first. I'll get my wrap.

MARY. Can I help you?

MRS. DRAPER. No. I know right where it is. (*She exits into room* D. L.)

HARDY. (*To* MARY.) I'll say good night, Mrs. Matthews.

MARY. (*Shaking hands.*) Good night. It was very nice having you here.

HARDY. (*To* GRANT *at* C.) I hope to hear from you on that.

GRANT. You'll be in touch with Jim.

HARDY. Just keep in mind what I said. Our funds are our secret

86

weapon. If an employer knows how much we've got in the bank, he knows just how long we can stay out on strike. We can't afford to open our books.

GRANT. (*Smiling.*) As an employer I can understand that. Of course, I have to show my books.

HARDY. (*Smiling sheepishly.*) Well, good night. Good night, Mrs. Matthews. See you in Washington, Senator. (HARDY *exits* U. L.)

SENATOR. (*Crossing to* MARY. CONOVER *crosses* D. R.) What you said about Sam Parrish—I can't wait to get back to Washington to tell it on him.—(*Turns to* GRANT.) Good night, Mr. Matthews. —(*Draws him down* L.) Look, will you promise me this? Before you speak in the Middle West again, will you have another talk with me—and I'd like to have Ed O'Neil and Earl Smith there. We can handle the farm problems in Congress, but we'd like to be sure we won't run into any vetoes.

GRANT. (*Laughing.*) Vetoes! Senator, you're moving a little too fast for me. I haven't even started to work on my inaugural address.

MARY. (*Trying to take part—moving from behind couch to* L. *of it.*) Inaugural address! My, that makes me nervous—and excited!

CONOVER. I'll be there holding your hand, Mary.

SENATOR. Jim, I know everything's safe in your hands. (*We hear a laugh from dining-room.*) Good night, Mr. Matthews. (*He shakes hands with* GRANT.) Good night, Mrs. Matthews. (KAY *and* ALEXANDER *enter from arch* R.) Good night, everybody! (SENATOR *exits* L.)

KAY. (*Entering.*) I'll remember that, Judge, the next time I'm in New Orleans.

ALEXANDER. Where's Lulubelle?

MRS. DRAPER. (*Who has just entered with wrap from door* L.) She's in the bedroom getting her things.

KAY. (*Crossing* MRS. DRAPER *downstage to door* L.) I'd better get mine. (*She exits into* L. *room.*)

ALEXANDER. My coat is out there, isn't it? (*He indicates hall and exits into it.*)

MRS. DRAPER. (*Crossing to* MARY L. *of sofa.*) It was so nice meeting you, Mrs. Matthews.

MARY. (*Shaking hands with* MRS. DRAPER.) Thank you. I hope we see each other soon.

87

MRS. DRAPER. You don't mind my falling in love with your husband, do you?

MARY. I don't see how you could help it.

MRS. DRAPER. (*To* GRANT.) I hope you and Jim get together on everything.

GRANT. Whoever the candidate is, you're going to be very valuable to him. I realize that. (KAY *enters from room* L., *with wrap, and crosses to behind chair* L. C.)

MRS. DRAPER. Well, if there's one group I do know how to swing, it's the foreigners. I don't pretend to be an intellectual, but since our so-called great minds have gotten us into the United Nations, we can't overlook the political advantage it gives us. Remember, there are lots of voters who are afraid of Russia!—and you'd be surprised how many people hate the British!

GRANT. I don't think we can capitalize on that, Mrs. Draper. We can't build world peace on hate. We have a certain leadership in the United Nations. We have to be very jealous of it.

KAY. Yes, but, Grant, if the party's to win, remember each nationality in America will be thinking of their home country. We can use that. (*To* CONOVER.) Am I right, Jim?

CONOVER. In Jersey City, Mayor Hague promised the Italians we'd rebuild Italy!

KAY. Exactly!

MRS. DRAPER. We've got to promise them that, and more, too.

CONOVER. It's bound to be part of the campaign. I don't see how we can very well avoid it. (*He has been eyeing* MARY *and now speaks to her.*) Do you, Mary?

MARY. (*Taking time to swallow.*) Well, some of the Democrats are being pretty open about it. (*She smiles at* CONOVER.)

MRS. DRAPER. I do have to run. Good-bye, Mr. Matthews. You'll find I'm right about all this! (*She shakes hands with* GRANT. *To* MARY.) Good night, Mrs. Matthews. It was a wonderful dinner— (*She crosses to arch* L.) and such good talk! (MRS. DRAPER *exits* U. L., *followed by* MARY. KAY *crosses to sofa* R. *and sits down* C. LULUBELLE *enters from bedroom* L. JUDGE ALEXANDER *enters from arch* L.)

ALEXANDER. (*Crossing to* GRANT.) Mr. Matthews, I just happened to find in my overcoat pocket here a little pamphlet. It's a reprint of some of my most important decisions. I thought you might like to look it over. (*He hands pamphlet to* GRANT.)

GRANT. I'll be very glad to study it.

ALEXANDER. And I think I can safely promise you the votes of five Southern States.

GRANT. (*Unbelieving.*) In the election?

ALEXANDER. Hell, no!—in the convention! (*He crosses to arch* L.)

LULUBELLE. (*Crossing to* GRANT.) Mr. Matthews, I can't tell you how crazy I am about that wife of yours. And that reminds me— (*She offers her hand to shake.*) Congratulations!

GRANT. Congratulations? I don't think the Democrats have conceded yet.

LULUBELLE. No, I mean on your anniversary—your weddin' anniversary! (GRANT *looks a bit blank, then it comes to him.*)

GRANT. Oh, yes, of course! Well, thank you! (*He shakes hands vigorously with* LULUBELLE. SAM *and* SPIKE *enter from arch* R.)

SAM. Spike, I hate to bother you with it. . . .

ALEXANDER. (*To* GRANT, *from arch* L.) Remember, when you speak in New Orleans, you're to be our house guest.

LULUBELLE. Good night, Mr. Matthews. But if you campaign through the South you'd better change your name from Grant to Lee! (LULUBELLE *and* ALEXANDER *exit through arch* L.)

SPIKE. (*To* CONOVER.) Jim, I'm going to try to switch Sam to your train tomorrow. You're on the Congressional, aren't you?

CONOVER. Yes.

SPIKE. (*To* SAM.) Better give me your space. (SAM *hands* SPIKE *railroad envelope.* SPIKE *sits* L. *end of sofa and starts figuring.*)

CONOVER. Yes, that's fine, Sam. I think on the way down we can have a pretty definite talk.

SPIKE. I'll get to work on it in the morning. (MARY *enters from* L. *arch.*)

SAM. (*Crossing to* L. *end of sofa.*) Well, I've got to catch up on my beauty sleep. Can I drop you, Mrs. Thorndyke?

GRANT. (*Crossing down* L. *of* SAM.) I'm going over to Jim's hotel with him. We can drop Mrs. Thorndyke. It's on the way.

SAM. Grant, the evening turned out fine. It was a great idea getting all these people together. Must have been something of an education for you. You see, Grant, you have to run your politics the same way you run your business. It's a question of taking practical measures. (MARY *has come down to* R. *of chair.* CONOVER *is far* R. *watching* MARY.)

GRANT. Sam, you'd better go home. You know you rile me. Pretty soon we'll be in an argument. (GRANT *gives* SAM *an affectionate push, which brings* SAM *to* L. *of* GRANT *and* R. *of* MARY.)

SAM. You're in a spot now where you can't indulge in any more of that radical talk. My God, look at the effect it's had on Mary!

GRANT. Sam, if you have nightmares, I'll bet they're all about Henry Wallace!

SAM. (*Remembering something.*) Oh, say!—Hilda'd never forgive me if I forgot to show you this. (*He takes a leather picture case from his pocket.*) Look! It's Bobby, taken in Japan. Made a hell of a record—sixteen Jap planes.

GRANT. (*Looking at picture,* MARY *also looks.*) You must be very proud of Bobby, Sam!

SAM. He wants to go right into the business. And I'm going to let him. Want to train him. I haven't got too many more years left. I want to leave him the soundest business in these whole United States. (*To* MARY *with almost pathetic justification.*) That isn't anything to be ashamed of, is it, Mary?

MARY. (*Pats* SAM, *and turns away.*) Give Bobby my love—and next time bring Hilda.

SAM. Good night, Mary. (*He kisses* MARY *and shakes hands with* GRANT.)

SPIKE. I'll leave your ticket at the hotel in the morning. (JENNY *enters from arch* R. *with tray.*)

SAM. See you on the train, Jim.

CONOVER. Good night, Sam. (SAM *exits.*)

GRANT. (*To* JENNY.) Jenny, will you ask Swenson to bring down my coat? I left it upstairs. (JENNY *exits behind* C. GRANT *crosses to ottoman* R. *and sits down.*)

KAY. Spike, why don't you get Jim's coat? (SPIKE *rises and starts for arch* L. SWENSON *crosses back and goes upstairs.*)

CONOVER. Well, Grant, you're still alive. I know you didn't look forward to this evening—but it wasn't so tough, was it?

GRANT. They certainly don't mind asking for heaven and earth, do they?

CONOVER. They don't expect to get heaven.

SPIKE. (*At arch* L.) No, they'll settle for the earth. (SPIKE *exits into hall* L. MARY *sits on arm of chair* L. C.)

KAY. I was pretty frank with them. I told them there were some things they just couldn't ask Mr. Matthews to do. They were pretty reasonable—on the whole. Of course, there's no question about it—we'll have to meet them halfway. (*She sees* GRANT *looking at her and smiles at him.*) Part way, at least.

90

CONOVER. I'll get all these people alone. They know they can't get too tough with me. Of course there are some points we'll have to concede. We can't get through life without conceding some things, can we, Mary? (*He crosses to* MARY *and puts his arm around her shoulder as if in reminder, but doesn't wait for an answer.* SPIKE *enters with* CONOVER'S *coat.*) I think all the Senator wanted to know was that Grant wouldn't fight the farm bloc. Hell, we all know we can't fight the farm bloc. They're too powerful. (SPIKE *helps* JIM *into his coat.*)

GRANT. I'm afraid, Jim, that when it comes to concessions, the Senator and his crowd will have to make some. (SWENSON *enters with* GRANT'S *coat and hat on stairs* U. L.) They want a floor under farm prices, but no ceiling. They can't have it both ways. (SPIKE *crosses* R. *in front of fireplace.*)

CONOVER. Oh, there's always a margin of give-and-take. We won't have any trouble there.

GRANT. (*Getting into his coat,* C.) Don't wait up, Swenson. I'm going to be late. (*He hands* SWENSON *the* JUDGE'S *pamphlet.*) And throw this away, will you? (*To the* OTHERS.) Well, we'd better get going.

SPIKE. I don't think the Senator is going to be half as tough as Mrs. Draper. I started kidding her. I said it was too bad we couldn't dig up Hitler. There might be some votes in it. (*He chuckles.*) She didn't know whether I was on the level or not. And from her answer, I don't know whether *she* was on the level or not.

GRANT. (*Buttoning up his coat.*) If you ask me, I don't think she was kidding. (*To* CONOVER.) I can't go whole hog with her, Jim.

CONOVER. (*Crossing to* GRANT.) Of course she goes overboard— but you can't dismiss the fact that those issues are coming up, and we've got to find some way of making a play for the foreign vote.

KAY. We know that every nation is going to feel the peace terms have done them an injustice. We can make a perfectly honest appeal for justice, and if that gets us some votes—I don't think we should quibble.

GRANT. Which are you thinking of first, the votes or the justice?

CONOVER. Grant, we can't help ourselves. The Democrats are going to play that side of the street—they're doing it already. Mary agrees with us on that. (*He has been watching* MARY. *She,*

91

instead of making any comment, rises and starts for stairway in hall.) We can find some way to take a stand for justice and still appeal to the foreign vote—and with a clear conscience. Don't you think so, Mary? (MARY *turns in* L. *arch.*)

MARY. No. I don't. I was trying to get out of the room before I got sick, but you wouldn't let me! I've sat here listening to you making plans for Grant to trade away the peace of the world to get a few votes! Now that we're in the United Nations let's use it!—use it to get the Italian votes and the Polish votes—let's use it to get the votes of those who hate the Russians and those who hate the British! How long is it going to be before you ask us to forgive Germany to get the German vote?

CONOVER. *(Warningly.)* Mary! ——

MARY. *(Crossing to back of chair* L. C.) You heard Mrs. Draper and how much did it mean to you? " She's a little overboard."— *(To* GRANT.) "You can't quite go whole hog with her!" And you heard Kay, too, cheering her on! None of you had the guts to come out and tell them they're starting another war, and to slap them down for it!

KAY. Now, Grant! Really!

CONOVER. Mary, do you know what you're doing?

MARY. Yes, Jim, I know what I'm doing! Look at Sam—he wants to leave a fortune to Bobby. What kind of a world is he going to leave to Bobby? The kind he wants isn't good enough for my children. Don't you know what's happened in the world? Are you willing to trust the people you brought here tonight with atomic power?

CONOVER. *(Harshly.)* We may not be as bright as you are, Mary, but the people here tonight were pretty representative.

MARY. Representative of what? Nobody represented the American people! They don't even represent the Republican Party. You represent what's dead in the Republican Party . . . and what's dead in the Democratic Party!

KAY. For heaven's sake, Mary, have a little faith in Grant.

MARY. What have *you* got faith in? The people? You're afraid to let them know what Grant really thinks. Don't you *believe* in Democracy?

KAY. *(Sharply, crossing to* C.) Why do you suppose we were here tonight? What do you think we were doing? All we were planning was the next election.

MARY. Yes, I know. Everybody here tonight was thinking of the

92

next election. Well, it's time somebody began thinking of the next generation. (*She covers her face with her hands, sobbing as she runs upstairs. There is a pause.*)

KAY. Well! . . . (*She turns to look at* GRANT. CONOVER *is also watching him.* GRANT *is standing in thought, without moving. There is another pause.*) I think we could all use a drink. Let's go over to my apartment and go to work on some highballs. (*There is another pause as they wait for* GRANT *to break away from his thoughts.*)

CONOVER. Grace Draper will do what I tell her to do. But we have some things to settle. I want to be able to kid these people along.

GRANT. I'm not going to kid anybody along. I never have.

KAY. (*Pleading.*) Grant, everybody here tonight was thinking of the future—which is how to get you elected. It's stupid right now to think in any other terms. (GRANT *unbuttons his overcoat and throws it and hat on sofa.* KAY *turns to* CONOVER *in alarm.*)

CONOVER. (*Crossing to* GRANT.) Grant, I've got to talk to those people, and that means you've got to talk to me!

GRANT. I'm talking to a lot of people in my speech Thursday night —you'll be one of them. I promised myself when I went into this that I would appeal to the best in the American people. The only advice I have ever had from any of you was to appeal to their worst.

CONOVER. I see you're the only honest man in politics.

GRANT. No, Jim, we have some damn good men. There are some wonderful men in the Senate, and in the House, too—Democrats and Republicans. But damn it, Jim, there aren't enough of them to shape the Party policies! The President of the United States is the one man elected to protect the welfare of this country as a whole. You want a candidate who will make deals with every special interest just to get votes. I can't play that game, Jim, so I'm afraid I can't be of any interest to you.

KAY. Well, Grant, I'm not going to accept that decision. (CONOVER *throws a look to* KAY, *then goes* U. C. *and turns as* KAY *crosses to* GRANT.) Oh, Grant, we've always talked these things out together. All right, we won't discuss it any more tonight. You're upset. (*She crosses to arch* L. *and turns.*) I'll be in touch with you tomorrow. Come on, Jim. (*She starts to exit and turns back.*) Be sure to tell Mary it was a charming evening. (KAY *exits.*)

CONOVER. I think Kay's right, Grant. You'd better sleep on it. I can stay over for another day.

93

GRANT. No, Jim. I've made up my mind.

CONOVER. Well, Grant, you're wrong. In this country we play politics—and to play politics you have to play ball. (CONOVER *starts out.*)

GRANT. (*Crossing* L.) I'm sorry, Jim. I've become very fond of you.

CONOVER. (*From arch* L.) Oh, don't send flowers. It's not my funeral. (CONOVER *exits.*)

SPIKE. (*After a pause.*) Mr. Matthews, will you marry me?

GRANT. (*Laughing.*) Be careful, Spike, I'm in the mood for it! I've never felt so relieved in my life. Thank God that's settled. I hope they're all listening in Thursday night! I'm going to burn their ears off. Any candidate for any office who threatens world peace for the sake of a few votes—there's the international criminal for you, Spike. I'll take care of them Thursday night—and from now on!

SPIKE. (*Crossing to* C.) You know, Jim may have to take you on your own terms.

GRANT. No, Spike, it's all over but the shouting—but oh boy, am I going to shout! (GRANT *crosses* D. R., *taking off his jacket, throws it on sofa, rolls up his shirt-sleeves.* MARY *enters down stairs, is surprised to find* GRANT *and* SPIKE *there.* GRANT *pays no attention to her, he is busy with his thoughts.*)

MARY. I thought you were gone. Where's Jim?

SPIKE. I think he's wiring Prof. Eisenhower.

GRANT. (*Pacing* R. *above sofa into bar.*) We've got to run business on a different basis . . .

MARY. What's happened?

SPIKE. Quiet, please, we're on the air.

GRANT. (*Crossing to* C.) Sam and his type are dead. They want to go back to something they've had before. We've got to move on to something we've NEVER had before. And I'm going to tell off the Senator, too . . . (*Crosses* L. *to* MARY.) It's time somebody spoke up for the farmers. The American farmer is not the unpatriotic, selfish, grasping bastard the farm bloc makes him out to be. Thank God, I can speak my mind now —— (*He looks back at* SPIKE.) I don't have to worry about being a candidate!

SPIKE. Now you're on the beam. Talk as though you're not a candidate and I think they'll have to make you one.

GRANT. Forget it, Spike. (*He crosses to* SPIKE *at* C. *and shakes hands.*) It's been great working with you. But it's all over. I'll be seeing you. This isn't good-bye.

SPIKE. You're damn right it isn't good-bye. I'll be around first thing Friday morning. (*He crosses to arch* L.) See you later, Mary.

GRANT. No, Spike, it's cold. But I'm in a great spot for my speech Thursday night. I haven't any commitments.

SPIKE. (*At arch* L.) You've got one.

GRANT. What?

SPIKE. You promised not to make me Postmaster General. But I'll tell you what I'm doing, Grant—I'm releasing you from that. I'll be Postmaster General. (SPIKE *exits* L.)

MARY. But, Grant, what happened?

GRANT. Mary, I'm not running for President. But that doesn't mean I'm out of politics. Nobody can afford to be out of politics. I'm going to be yelling from the sidelines; you've got to be yelling; everybody's got to be yelling. I'm going to be in there asking questions, and I'm going to see that the people get the answers.

MARY. There are a lot of questions to ask, Grant. You're going to be a busy man.

GRANT. (*Crossing to* D. R.) You're damned right I'll be busy. Busy? Say, I didn't do a real job in any one of my plants. Let's make the trip all over again.

MARY. (*Crossing down* C.) But, Grant, you need a rest first. We both do.

GRANT. All right, what do you say we go back to Victoria?

MARY. Victoria?

GRANT. Say—do you know something? (*He crosses to* MARY, *shaking finger at her.*) You forgot this is our wedding anniversary!

MARY. (*Pretending surprise.*) I did? Oh, damn it all to hell! (GRANT *smacks* MARY *on the behind.*)

GRANT. Cut that out, Maizie! (*The realization comes to* MARY *that he has smacked her and called her "Maizie." Her face lights up.* GRANT *paces below sofa* R. *then around above it and stops.*) Darling, (MARY *turns to him.*) you're right about the future. (*He starts toward* MARY.) We've got something great to work for! (CURTAIN *begins to fall as he reaches* MARY *and enfolds her in his arms.*)

THE END

95

PROPERTY PLOT

ACT I—SCENE 1—ON STAGE

Mahogany table desk
  Bookends
  5 books
  Large blotter
  Loose papers
  Copy of " Who's Who "
  Silver inkstand
  2 inkwells
  Pens
  Telephone
  Note pad container
  Ashtray
  Cigarette box
  Cigarettes
  Matches
  Small tole lamp (elec.)
  Waste-basket (under desk)
Large red leather armchair (R. of desk)
Side chair (L. of desk)
Side chair (R. of console table)

Armchair (D. L. of console table)
End table (R. of armchair)
  Ashtray
  Cigarette box
  Matches
  Empty highball glass
End table (L. of door)
  Bowl of flowers
Console table (L. wall)
  Cigarette box
  Cigarettes
  Ashtray
  Tole tray
    3 highball glasses
    Ice-cube bowl
    Ice
    Small bottle White Rock
    1 bottle Scotch
    3 full decanters in silver set
  Lamp (elec.)

ACT I—SCENE 1—OFFSTAGE

Slip of paper—Norah
Slip of paper—Spike
Pencils—Spike

Wrist-watch—Grant
Handbag and mirror—Kay
Hat—Spike

ACT I—SCENE 2—ON STAGE

Chest of drawers (above window)
2 upholstered chairs—D. L. (removable back and seat cushions)
End table (between chairs above)
  Cigarette lighter
  Cigarettes
  Cigarette box
  Matches
  Ashtray

Side chair (R. of door U. L. C.)
Double studio bed
  Upholstered headboard (removable)
  Spread
  White blanket (folded on top of spread)
  White blanket ⎱ sewn together
  Top sheet ⎰
  Bottom sheet

96

Mattress pad
Mattress
2 pillows
2 pillow slips
Bell cord with push button (hangs L. side of bed)
Light switch—(R. of door U. L. C.)
2 end tables (R. and L. of bed) —each with:
Lamp
Ashtray
Small vase of flowers
Telephone—(end table L. of bed)
Small upholstered bench (foot of bed)
Matching side chair (at desk)

Table desk:
Small lamp
Blotter
Envelope holder
Envelopes and stationery
Calendar
Small blotter
China cigarette box
China ashtray
Pencils
Inkstand
Inkwell
Quill pen (in small glass holder)
20 pages typewritten script
Paper knife
Waste-basket (under desk)

ACT I—SCENE 2—OFFSTAGE

Small silver tray—Stevens, L.
2 Scotch highballs—Stevens, L.
1 pr. glasses, Chinese style— Norah, L.
1 pr. steel rim glasses—to wear— Norah, L.
1 print dress—pressed—on hanger —Norah, L.

1 duplicate print dress—UN-pressed—Norah, R.
2 women's suitcases ⎱
1 woman's hat box ⎰ Norah, L.
Cigarette case—Grant
Cigarettes—Grant
Cigarette lighter—Grant
Horn-rimmed glasses—Grant

ACT II—ON STAGE

Side chair (above door D. R.)
Small double door chest (R. wall)
Vase of flowers
Desk (back wall R. of alcove)
Blotter
Phone (no dial)
Small blotter
Inkstand with inkwell
Matches
Pen
Stationery and envelope holder
Stationery and envelopes
Small lamp

Side chair (at desk)
Small console table (R. wall of alcove)
Light switch (R. of door U. C.)
Sofa
2 end tables (each end of sofa)
2 lamps (on end tables)
Ashtray (R. end table)
Small armchair (D. L. of sofa)
Chest of drawers (L. wall)
Picture (over chest of drawers)
Basket of fruit (on chest of drawers)

(All Offstage Props Act II work off u. c.)

Coins—Conover
Bills—Grant
2 Detroit newspapers — " Free Press," " News "—Spike
Several slips of paper—Spike
Pencils—Spike
Mary's luggage from Act I— Scene 2—Bellhop
2 pieces man's airplane luggage— Bellhop
Radio battery set with elec. cord —Bellhop
100 telegrams (25 out of envelopes)—Grant
Cigarette—Kay
Cigarettes—Grant
Cigarette case—Grant
Cigarette lighter—Grant
Cigarettes (in handbag)—Mary
Cigar—Conover
Silver tray
  2 Martinis
  1 Old Fashioned
  1 jigger of Scotch
  1 highball glass with ice
  1 small White Rock
  1 bottle-opener
  1 waiter's check
  Pencil
} No. 1 setup for Waiter

Service table on wheels
Silver tray with:
  1 Martini
  3 cups
  3 saucers
  3 butters
  3 forks
  3 knives
  6 spoons
  3 napkins
} No. 2 setup for Waiter
Table-cloth
Portable oven
  3 plates
  3 hamburgers (1 with onions)
  3 vegetables
Napkins on top of oven (to handle plates)
} No. 3 setup for Waiter
Silver tray
  Silver coffee pot
  1 dish chocolate ice-cream
  1 waiter's check
  Pencil
} No. 4 setup for Waiter

ACT III—SCENE 1—ON STAGE

Fireplace mantel (R. wall)
Bowl of flowers (on mantel)
Grate (in fireplace)
Mirror (wall above mantel)
End table (above mantel)
Silver ashtray (on above)
End table (below fireplace)
Lamps (on both of above end tables)

Hassock (D. L. of fireplace)
Sofa (R. C.)
2 pillows on sofa
Bar (beyond arch R.)
  6 liquor bottles (top R. end of bar, including Haig & Haig)
  Tray of ten (10) Sazaracs (underneath bar)

Tray with:
2 Highballs ⎫
2 Manhattans ⎬ top L. end
1 Coca-Cola ⎭ of bar
Various liquor bottles (wall cup-
board behind bar)
2 cushioned bar stools (front of
bar)
Mahogany dresser (c. of back
wall between arches)
Large vase of flowers (on
dresser)
Large portrait of Mary Matthews
and children (wall above
dresser)
2 pedestals (either side of dresser)
2 lamps (on pedestals)
2 end chairs (R. and L. of pedestals)

End table (L. wall foot of stairs)
—double from 11.
Tray of hors d'oeuvres (on above
end table)
Highboy (L. wall)
Vase of greenery (on highboy)
2 large upholstered club chairs
(D. L. C.)
End table (between above chairs)
—double from 11
Silver ashtray
Silver cigarette cup
Silver ashtray—(on dresser U. C.)
Silver cigarette cup
Push button (in wall above door
frame D. L.)
Wrapped liquor bottle (on floor
front of sofa)
Silver ashtray (on sofa — for
Spike)

ACT III—SCENES 1 and 2—OFFSTAGE

Silver tray with: ⎫
3 Martinis ⎬ Swenson—
2 Highballs ⎭ off R. (31)
Silver tray with: ⎫
3 Martinis ⎬ Swenson—
4 Manhattans ⎭ off R. (31)
Silver tray with:
Coffee pot ⎫
Postum for coffee ⎬ Swenson
Bourbon and soda ⎭ off R. (32)
2 demitasse cups— ⎫
1 full—1 empty ⎪
2 demitasse saucers ⎬ Props off L.
2 demitasse spoons ⎪
¼ full Sazarac ⎭

Empty silver tray—Jenny—off R.
Diagram—on piece of cardboard
—Spike—off R.
Scratch pad—Swenson—off R.
Pencil—Swenson—off R.
Pencil—Spike—off R.
Photo in small leather ⎫
folder—32 ⎪
Finance papers—31 ⎬ Sam—
R. R. tickets in R. R. ⎪ off L.
envelope—32 ⎪
Pencils ⎭
Wrapped cigar box — Grant —
off L.
Pamphlet—Judge—off L.

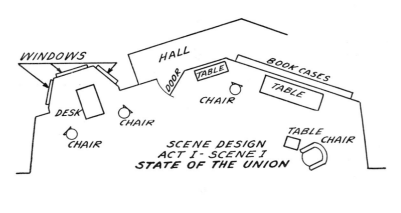

WINDOWS

HALL

DOOR

TABLE

BOOK CASES

TABLE

CHAIR

DESK

CHAIR

CHAIR

TABLE

CHAIR

SCENE DESIGN
ACT I - SCENE I
STATE OF THE UNION

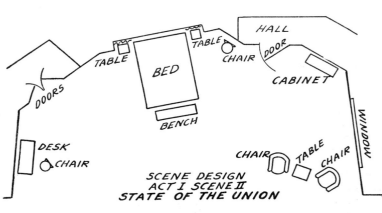

HALL

DOOR

TABLE

TABLE

CHAIR

CABINET

BED

DOORS

WINDOW

BENCH

DESK

CHAIR

CHAIR

TABLE

CHAIR

SCENE DESIGN
ACT I SCENE II
STATE OF THE UNION

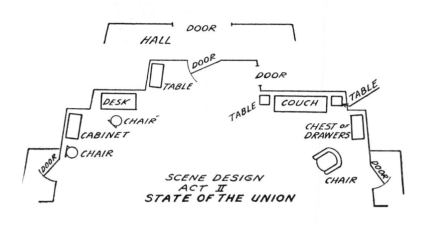

SCENE DESIGN
ACT II
STATE OF THE UNION

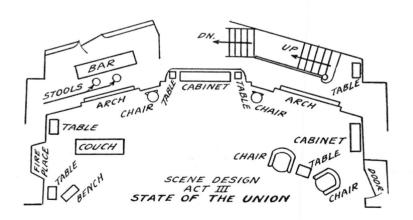

SCENE DESIGN
ACT III
STATE OF THE UNION

101

TODAY'S HOTTEST NEW PLAYS

❑ **THREE VIEWINGS by Jeffrey Hatcher.** Three comic-dramatic monologues, set in a midwestern funeral parlor, interweave as they explore the ways we grieve, remember, and move on. *"Finally, what we have been waiting for: a new, true, idiosyncratic voice in the theater. And don't tell me you hate monologues; you can't hate them more than I do. But these are much more: windows into the deep of each speaker's fascinating, paradoxical, unique soul, and windows out into a gallery of surrounding people, into hilarious and horrific coincidences and conjunctions, into the whole dirty but irresistible business of living in this damnable but spellbinding place we presume to call the world."* - New York Magazine. [1M, 2W]

❑ **HAVING OUR SAY by Emily Mann.** The Delany Sisters' Bestselling Memoir is now one of Broadway's Best-Loved Plays! Having lived over one hundred years apiece, Bessie and Sadie Delany have plenty to say, and their story is not simply African-American history or women's history...it is our history as a nation. *"The most provocative and entertaining family play to reach Broadway in a long time."* - New York Times. *"Fascinating, marvelous, moving and forceful."* - Associated Press. [2W]

❑ **THE YOUNG MAN FROM ATLANTA Winner of the 1995 Pulitzer Prize. by Horton Foote.** An older couple attempts to recover from the suicide death of their only son, but the menacing truth of why he died, and what a certain Young Man from Atlanta had to do with it, keeps them from the peace they so desperately need. *"Foote ladles on character and period nuances with a density unparalleled in any living playwright."* - NY Newsday. [5M, 4W]

❑ **SIMPATICO by Sam Shepard.** Years ago, two men organized a horse racing scam. Now, years later, the plot backfires against the ringleader when his partner decides to come out of hiding. *"Mr. Shepard writing at his distinctive, savage best."* - New York Times. [3M, 3W]

❑ **MOONLIGHT by Harold Pinter.** The love-hate relationship between a dying man and his family is the subject of Harold Pinter's first full-length play since *Betrayal. "Pinter works the language as a master pianist works the keyboard."* - New York Post. [4M, 2W, 1G]

❑ **SYLVIA by A.R. Gurney.** This romantic comedy, the funniest to come along in years, tells the story of a twenty-two year old marriage on the rocks, and of Sylvia, the dog who turns it all around. *"A delicious and dizzy new comedy."* - New York Times. *"FETCHING! I hope it runs longer than Cats!"* - New York Daily News. [2M, 2W]

DRAMATISTS PLAY SERVICE, INC.
440 Park Avenue South, New York, New York 10016 212-683-8960 Fax 212-213-1539

TODAY'S HOTTEST NEW PLAYS

❏ **MOLLY SWEENEY by Brian Friel, Tony Award-Winning Author of** *Dancing at Lughnasa.* Told in the form of monologues by three related characters, *Molly Sweeney* is mellifluous, Irish storytelling at its dramatic best. Blind since birth, Molly recounts the effects of an eye operation that was intended to restore her sight but which has unexpected and tragic consequences. *"Brian Friel has been recognized as Ireland's greatest living playwright. Molly Sweeney confirms that Mr. Friel still writes like a dream. Rich with rapturous poetry and the music of rising and falling emotions...Rarely has Mr. Friel written with such intoxicating specificity about scents, colors and contours."* - New York Times. [2M, 1W]

❏ **SWINGING ON A STAR (The Johnny Burke Musical) by Michael Leeds. 1996 Tony Award Nominee for Best Musical.** The fabulous songs of Johnny Burke are perfectly represented here in a series of scenes jumping from a 1920s Chicago speakeasy to a World War II USO Show and on through the romantic high jinks of the Bob Hope/Bing Crosby "Road Movies." Musical numbers include such favorites as "Pennies from Heaven," "Misty," "Ain't It a Shame About Mame," "Like Someone in Love," and, of course, the Academy Award winning title song, "Swinging on a Star." *"A WINNER. YOU'LL HAVE A BALL!"* - New York Post. *"A dazzling, toe-tapping, finger-snapping delight!"* - ABC Radio Network. *"Johnny Burke wrote his songs with moonbeams!"* - New York Times. [3M, 4W]

❏ **THE MONOGAMIST by Christopher Kyle.** Infidelity and mid-life anxiety force a forty-something poet to reevaluate his 60s values in a late 80s world. *"THE BEST COMEDY OF THE SEASON. Trenchant, dark and jagged. Newcomer Christopher Kyle is a playwright whose social satire comes with a nasty, ripping edge - Molière by way of Joe Orton."* - Variety. *"By far the most stimulating playwright I've encountered in many a buffaloed moon."* - New York Magazine. *"Smart, funny, articulate and wisely touched with rue...the script radiates a bright, bold energy."* - The Village Voice. [2M, 3W]

❏ **DURANG/DURANG by Christopher Durang.** These cutting parodies of *The Glass Menagerie* and *A Lie of the Mind,* along with the other short plays in the collection, prove once and for all that Christopher Durang is our theater's unequivocal master of outrageous comedy. *"The fine art of parody has returned to theater in a production you can sink your teeth and mind into, while also laughing like an idiot."* - New York Times. *"If you need a break from serious drama, the place to go is Christopher Durang's silly, funny, over-the-top sketches."* - TheatreWeek. [3M, 4W, flexible casting]

DRAMATISTS PLAY SERVICE, INC.
440 Park Avenue South, New York, New York 10016 212-683-8960 Fax 212-213-1539